SUSPENDED PASSION

THE FRENCH LIST

RECENT TITLES FROM THE FRENCH LIST

ROLAND BARTHES
Essays and Interviews
Volume 1: 'A Very Fine Gift' and Other Writings on Theory
Volume 2: 'The Scandal of Marxism' and Other Writings on Politics
Volume 3: 'Masculine, Feminine, Neuter' and Other Writings on Literature
Volume 4: Signs and Images. Writings on Art, Cinema and Photography
Volume 5: 'Simply a Particular Contemporary'. Interviews, 1970–79

DOMINIQUE EDDÉ
The Crime of Jean Genet

RENÉ CHAR
'The Inventors' and Other Poems
Hypnos: Notes from the French Resistance, 1944–45

YVES BONNEFOY
The Anchor's Long Chain
Rue Traversière

PASCAL QUIGNARD
Abysses
The Sexual Night

ANTONIN ARTAUD
50 Drawings to Murder Magic

GEORGES PERROS
Paper Collage

MARGUERITE DURAS

SUSPENDED PASSION

Interviews with Leopoldina Pallotta della Torre

TRANSLATED BY CHRIS TURNER

LONDON NEW YORK CALCUTTA

PAP
TAGORE
www.bibliofrance.in

This work is published via the Publication Assistance Programme Tagore,
with support of Institut français en Inde / Ambassade de France en Inde
and the Institut français de Paris

Seagull Books, 2016

Published in French as *La Passion suspendue*
© Editions du Seuil, 2013

English translation © Chris Turner, 2016

First published in English translation by Seagull Books, 2016

ISBN 978 0 8574 2 329 0

British Library Cataloguing-in-Publication Data
A catalogue record for this book is available from the British Library.

Typeset by Seagull Books, Calcutta, India
Printed and bound by Maple Press, York, Pennsylvania, USA

CONTENTS

I met Marguerite Duras for the first time in 1987, shortly after the Italian translation of *Blue Eyes, Black Hair* was published.

Getting that interview for *La Stampa* wasn't very easy.

To persuade her to do it, I had to call several times and haggle. She seemed in a state of weary indifference. Saying she had flu and complaining of a heavy workload (I discovered later that she was working on the screenplay of *The Lover*), she declined my invitation. Then, one afternoon, I mentioned my friendship with Inge Feltrinelli.[1] Thrown for a moment by that, she came back with: 'Get her to call me right away.' I rang Inge and begged her to call Duras. Half an hour later, I was inexplicably granted a meeting.

I turned up at rue Saint-Benoît a little ahead of time. The third-floor landing was tiny and poorly lit. I rang, but had to wait a few minutes before a male voice from behind the door (I immediately thought of Yann Andréa, the man she had been living with for nine years) suggested that I go and get a coffee in the café on the ground floor of the building and not come back for at least half an hour. From deep within the flat I heard Marguerite's voice—she was claiming she had forgotten this appointment for our interview.

Returning at the time specified, I was admitted to find her with her back to me. She was small, very small, and seated, as ever, in her dusty bedroom cluttered with papers and objects, her elbows propped on her writing table.

She stared at me in silence, not taking the slightest notice of what I was saying. Then she began to speak, painstakingly adopting that extraordinary timbre she is able to assume, modulating her tone and her pauses. From time to time she stopped, with some irritation, to clarify the words I had taken down in my notebook. And as soon as the telephone rang, she clasped my hand, clamping it in her own to prevent me from transcribing even a single word she spoke.

The whole time I was with her (three hours, perhaps more), she was constantly pulling large mints out of a drawer, choosing only at the end to offer me one.

When we were done, she even agreed to be photographed. Dressed in her usual 'Marguerite Duras uniform'—short, flared skirt, roll-neck pullover, black waistcoat, platform shoes—she turned around slowly to pose. It was as if she were defying the lens, ensuring that her blue eyes were in the picture, as well as the precious rings bedecking her fingers.

As I was leaving, I asked her if I could come back. 'Do as you like,' she said, 'but I don't have much time.'

I leant over to say goodbye and she kissed me.

As soon as I returned to Paris after the summer, I called her. I explained that I'd brought a nice piece of Parmesan back from Italy for her. It was noon and Marguerite had just got up. 'Good,' she said, 'as it happens, I had nothing to eat in the house.'

She suggested that I come over in a few minutes. However, on this occasion too, she wasn't the one who answered the door. As for the shy, conscientious Yann, he simply took my heavy package from me and as quickly closed the door in my face.

I realized that it wasn't the moment to press matters and I let a few days go by.

Long afternoons of chatting and conversation followed in that collusive intimacy that (perhaps inevitably) develops over time between two women.

It was in this way that our talk—her elliptical remarks—emerged, at times without any clear connection, to be re-organized and re-ordered subsequently. Then it would go on, interminably, for hours. Until Marguerite peremptorily announced, 'That's enough, now.'

And, as though he had been waiting for the signal, Yann would enter from another room, offering as usual to take her for a walk, and delicately help her on with her strawberry-coloured coat.

As she spoke, Marguerite was constantly tugging at the crumpled white skin of her face, then smoothing it out. She would take off the pair of men's spectacles she had worn since her younger days, then put them back on again.

I listened to her remembering, thinking, letting go and gradually relinquishing her natural wariness—egocentric, vain, stubborn, voluble. And yet capable, at times, of kind words and enthusiasms, of shyness, of suppressed and then uproarious laughter. She seemed suddenly fired with a consuming, voracious and almost childlike curiosity.

I can still remember the last time we met. As always, the television was on in another part of the living room and Marguerite's face seemed tired, as though it had swelled in the course of a few days.

She wanted to know everything about me. She couldn't stop asking questions—I had to tell her about my life, my loves or talk at great length about my mother, as she had about hers. 'To the end, my mother will remain the maddest, most unpredictable of the people I've met in my entire life,' she tells me with an already distant smile.

Leopoldina Pallotta della Torre

It was more than fifteen years ago, when I read Angelo Morino's essay on Marguerite Duras *Il cinese e Marguerite* (Palermo: Sellerio, 1997), that I learnt of the existence of this interview which was then still unpublished in France. In fact, Angelo Morino quoted copiously from it and it was immediately apparent that it contained elements that hadn't been covered at such length in the various interviews published in French. The fact that Leopoldina Pallotta della Torre was Italian, her very determination and insistence, her thematic organization and her highly structured thinking prevented a certain indulgence and the evasions one finds in most of the interviews published hitherto, in which interviewers are often led, by their high-handed interlocutor, to speak 'Duras'—a coded language with which all her admirers, imitators and detractors are familiar, a language they variously caricature or practise and in which, most importantly, the many digressions and unfinished trains of thought at times render the dialogue borderline incoherent or, at any rate, divert it from the topic and leave it confused.

As for Angelo Morino's book, it was a study of the genesis of *The Lover* and a detailed comparison of the biographical elements scattered throughout Duras' work, from *The Sea Wall* to *Yann Andréa Steiner*, and supposedly new ones contributed by the novel that considerably widened the author's audience. It raised doubts about the late 'revelation' made in that book regarding the identity of Huynh Thuy-Lê, the 'Chinese' lover, who takes the place of *The Sea Wall*'s 'Monsieur Jo'. Comparing the three versions of the same events that Duras offers in *The Sea Wall*, *The Lover* and *The North China Lover*, stressing the difference in the number of brothers and, particularly, the identity of the lover (from the French Monsieur Jo, he becomes Huynh Thuy-Lê, a Vietnamese with a Chinese father) and attempting, above all, to explain the very longstanding concealment of the 'truth', he puts forward the idea that *The Lover* recounts an episode in the life of Marguerite's mother, Marie Legrand, who is said, in his version, to have cheated on Henri (known as Émile) Donnadieu with a Vietnamese or Chinese man. Marguerite and her youngest brother Paulo would then be the children of that lover (there are numerous allusions in *The North China Lover* to the lover, the daughter and the youngest son having similar skin). Pierre, by contrast, would be the only son of Émile Donnadieu. This argument—that the Lover is the mother's lover, not the daughter's—is picked up by Michel Tournier in his book *Célébrations*.[1] It is an argument that would almost be persuasive were it not for Marguerite's physical resemblance to Émile Donnadieu in the photographs the writer has made public. Marguerite's gaze and the shape of her eyes come, in reality, from Émile Donnadieu. And in June 1998, by which time Duras was dead, Danielle Laurin published in *Lire* magazine the story of her meeting with a former classmate of Duras', Mme Ly, at Sa Dec. She attests to Marguerite's escapades with Huynh Thuy-Lê and states that in 1952, twenty years after Duras left Vietnam once and for all, she, Mme Ly, had received combs from Paris from her through Huynh Thuy-Lê's sister-in-law, which would imply that the writer was still in touch with her Chinese lover—or, at least, with his family. The house of Huynh Thuan, the lover's Chinese father, became a 'Lovers' Museum' in Sa Dec, though Duras never set foot in it. It is visited by tourists, who are also able to stay overnight.

Though Duras was by no means unwilling to give interviews and many important ones are available in book form—in particular, with Xavière Gauthier in *Les Parleuses* (Paris: Minuit, 1974), in *Le Camion* (Paris: Minuit, 1977), with Michelle Porte in *Les Lieux de Marguerite Duras* (Paris: Minuit, 1978), with Serge Daney and the *Cahiers du Cinéma* editorial team in *Les Yeux verts* (1987), with Jérôme Beaujour in *La Vie matérielle* (Paris: POL, 1987), with Pierre Dumayet in *Dits à la television* (Paris: EPEL, 1999), with Dominique Noguez in *La Couleur des mots* (Paris: Benoit Jacob, 2001), with François Mitterand in *Le Bureau de poste de la rue Dupin* (Paris: Gallimard, 2006) and with Jean-Pierre Ceton in *Entretiens* (Paris: Bourin, 2012)—and though, as her work progressed, she gave many to the press or to radio and television (with Alain Veinstein, Bernard Pivot, Bernard Rapp, Michelle Porte or Benoît Jacquot),[2] no interview project was undertaken in French that was comparable to the conversation with Leopoldina Pallotta della Torre, whose aim was to deal exhaustively with the writer's life and career in a single volume. Pallotta della Torre modelled her book on the interviews

Marguerite Yourcenar produced with Matthieu Galey, published as *With Open Eyes* (Boston: Beacon Press, 1980), a work she cites several times in her questions.

Since La Tartaruga, the publishers of the original book, had ceased operations, it was impossible to unearth a copy until I met Annalisa Bertoni, a teacher at the University of Limoges and the press attachée of the Italian publishers Portaparole. On the occasion of the publication of a little book I co-authored with Adriana Asti, *Se souvenir et oublier*, published by Portaparole (2011), I spoke to Annalisa Bertoni about these mythic lost interviews. It turned out that, having done her PhD on Duras' work, she had kept a copy.

Enquiries among friends in Italian publishing enabled me to track down Leopoldina Pallotta della Torre's family in Bologna. And I was ultimately able to obtain contact details for her in Lucca.

Clearly, in retranslating the words of a French writer from Italian, there is a danger that the way those words were expressed will be distorted. I have attempted, as far as is possible, to restore Duras' tone as it is familiar to her French readers. And to provide in the notes such additional information as seems useful, and any necessary rectifications.

I should like to express my gratitude here to Annalisa Bertoni, without whom this book would not have been available to a French audience.

René de Ceccatty

• • ENGLISH TRANSLATOR'S NOTE • •

Given the complex circumstances of this book's origin, the English translation has been based mainly on the French edition published by Éditions du Seuil in 2013, rather than the Italian edition published by La Tartaruga edizioni in 1989. Since access to the original French has not been possible, the French translator René de Ceccatty has generally been assumed to have fulfilled his mission of restoring Duras' 'tone' in the production of his text.

There are no footnotes in the Italian edition of these interviews and those which appear in this book are, therefore, generally the work of Monsieur de Ceccatty. On the rare occasions where a footnote is marked [Trans.], it has been supplied by me.

I would like to thank Professor Emeritus Leslie Hill of the University of Warwick for his assistance with some aspects of this project. Overall responsibility for the translation rests, of course, with me.

Chris Turner

• • • A CHILDHOOD • • •

・・・

*You were born at Gia Dinh, a few miles from Saigon, and, moving count-
less times with your family—to Vinh Long, Sa Dec, etc.—you lived
in Vietnam, which at that time was a French colony, until you were
eighteen. Do you think you had a special childhood?*

> I sometimes think the whole of my writing originates from
> there—between the paddy fields, the forests and the soli-
> tude. From that emaciated, lost child that I was, the white
> girl not from those parts, though more Vietnamese than
> French, always barefoot, with no regular hours or social
> graces, accustomed to watching the sun set slowly over the
> river, my face always thoroughly sunburnt.

How would you describe yourself as a child?

> I've always been small. No one ever said I was pretty. In our
> house, there was no mirror to see yourself in.

What relation is there between these strata of memory and your writing?

> I have overwhelming memories, memories so strong that
> they can never be evoked by writing. It's better that way,
> don't you think?

Your Indochinese childhood is an essential reference for your imagination.

My imagination will never be able to equal it in intensity. Stendhal's right—childhood has no end.

What are your oldest memories?

It's in the highlands, amid the smells of rain, jasmine and meat, that I locate the earliest years of my life. To us children, the exhausting afternoons in Indochina seemed to have in them that sense of a defiance of the stifling nature all around us.

A sense of mystery and the forbidden hung over the forest. We so enjoyed those days, my two brothers and I, when we ventured out, battling through the tangled creepers and orchids, in danger at any moment of coming across snakes or, I suppose, even tigers.

I talked about this at great length in *The Sea Wall*.

The superhuman calm and indescribable gentleness I was surrounded by have left indelible marks.

I found fault with God, of course, when I went by the lazarettos outside the villages—a vague impression of death floated over the hillsides all along the Siamese frontier where we lived. And yet I still have the melodious laughter of that people in my ears—the laughter that attested to an unwavering vitality.

What image do you have now, after all this time, of India and Indochina?

They are the core of the world's absurdity, a point where delirium, poverty, death, madness and life are all jumbled together.

The East you reconstructed in your books is a deliquescent, devastated place. I don't know to what extent it can be described as real.

I experienced it at the height of colonial times and I've never been back since.[1] Moreover, the veracity of so-called realism isn't my concern.

You grew up speaking French and Vietnamese. What influence did that experience of bilingualism have on you? What have you gained from knowing a culture so distant from the European?

For years I repressed a large part of that life. Then, suddenly, the things I went through in the unconsciousness of my first twelve years returned violently. The poverty, the fear, the forest darkness, the Ganges, the Mekong, the tigers, and the lepers I found terrifying, gathered by the side of the road fetching water, all came back to me whole. I felt my country was taking its revenge.

At a very early age you became used to moving about, to changing houses and moving from town to town.

That was on account of my father's job as a colonial civil servant. As a little girl, I never looked at the houses—at the objects or furniture in them. But then I knew them all, I could have travelled around them in the dark like an animal with my eyes closed. I remember there were places where you could escape to when you'd had enough of the grown-ups. Since that time, I've always been looking for a place and I've never managed to be where I would have wanted—a vagabond life, if I can put it that way.

A life in exile, even, since you left your native country for ever nearly fifty years ago.

I think that will condition the whole of my life. As with the Jews, everything I took away with me on my wanderings has become even more intense for being distant, absent.

In what way, as you see it, has this special childhood made you who you are?

There's still something wild in me, even now. A sort of animal attachment to life.

Books like The Lover *or* The Sea Wall *could, alternatively, be read as 'family portraits in an interior', as 'conversation pieces'. Before we come to the complex relationship with your mother, what were relations with your family like up to your teenage years?*

There was something both noble and coarse in the way we lived. It definitely wasn't a European or French upbringing. And there was no pretence, no recourse to the primal, aggressive instinct that governs families and binds them together. We all knew that we weren't destined to stay together for long—the family was there to guarantee our shared survival. We would soon be separated and begin to live our lives.

You don't think all that could have had a major influence on your future as a writer?

I took to writing to make the silence speak—that silence under which I'd been crushed. At twelve, that seemed to me the only way.

After the death of your father when you were four, you stayed with your mother and your two brothers.

Now that they're all dead, I can speak about them calmly. The pain has gone. The younger of my brothers had a thin, agile body. It reminded me, heaven knows why, of my first lover, the Chinese. He was silent and fearful and I didn't succeed in detaching myself from him until the day he died. The other brother was a bad lot, with no scruples or conscience—perhaps even no feelings. He was domineering and we were scared of him. These days, I still associate him with Robert Mitchum's character in *The Night of the Hunter*, a mix of paternal and criminal instincts. That, I think, is where the wariness I've always felt towards men comes from.

One of the last times I saw him, he came to my flat in Paris to take money from me. It was during the Occupation. My husband Robert Antelme was in a concentration camp. I found out many years later that he robbed my mother, too, and that he died alone in hospital, ravaged by alcohol.

In Agatha, *which you wrote for the theatre drawing on the plot of Robert Musil's* Man without Qualities, *you put the supposed incestuous love between Agatha and her brother Ulrich squarely on the stage.*

The ultimate stage of passion, yes. I was in denial for a long time about the passion that I might have felt, beneath my hatred, for my brother. It's the way he looked at me that convinced me it was real. When we were given a record player, I never wanted to dance with him. Contact with his body horrified me but at the same time I was attracted by it.

The figure of your brother appears in The Sea Wall *and in* The Lover.

It was only with *The Lover* that I managed to free myself of this hatred. When he became an electrician, in France, I stayed with the younger of my two brothers, my only bulwark against my mother's hysteria and tantrums. I suppose we weren't either of us the children she would have wanted.

Whole Days in the Trees is the story of an old lady who comes back to France after living many years in the colonies and meets up with her eldest son—a thief and a crook—who has always been her favourite.

Yes, indeed. Of the three of us, he was always the most loved. My mother felt guilty for making him jealous by giving him a brother and a sister.

And what was her attitude towards you?

She couldn't stand our exotic ways. She was constantly telling us we were French. She forced us to eat bread and honey when we preferred rice, fish and the mangoes we stole during her naps. At fifteen, people took me for a half-caste. I didn't rise to certain insults that came my way. So far as we knew, my mother had always been faithful to her husband, even when he left her on her own for months.

You've never spoken much about your father.

Perhaps because, without knowing it, it was for him that, as I've lived, I've continued to write. I lost and found men as though they had been my father. He was a teacher and wrote maths books. He died so early that I can say I never knew him. What I can see now are just his bright eyes, and at times I seem to feel them fixed on me. All I have of him is a faded photograph. My mother never talked to us about him.

What happened after he died?

We were very poor, and my mother so stubborn that she insisted on going her own sweet way. As a widow, she bought that piece of land, an unworkable paddy field, flooded by the Pacific, on which she worked to no avail for twenty years. After the wall built to hold back the sea collapsed, she never recovered—she more or less lost her wits. She kept saying we'd been abandoned by everyone, while the civil servants who'd sold us the land grew rich. She ended up alone, bitter and poor, after slaving like an animal. As an old woman, she went off to die by the river Loire—the only place where she could live, she said, now that the colonies were gone.

Les Impudents *and also* The Lover *and* The Sea Wall—*your mother reappears in your novels.*

The Sea Wall, as I remember, made her angry . . . My life was lived through my mother. She lived inside me to the point of obsession. I would have died in childhood, I think, if she'd died. I don't think I've ever recovered from the day, so long ago, when we parted.

What sort of woman was she?

Exuberant and mad, as only mothers can be. In existence, I think one's mother is, generally speaking, the strangest, most unpredictable and elusive person one meets. She was tall and tough, but always ready, nonetheless, to protect us from the aspects of that squalid life we were living.

She always dressed in old, worn-out clothes. And I can still see her pacing up and down the bedroom in her nightdress or in the shadows of the colonial dining room, screaming in despair that she didn't want to go back to France. She was the daughter of peasants from the Pas-de-Calais and, until the day she left the colonies, she refused to speak Vietnamese. And yet she taught in native schools and was certainly closer to the Vietnamese and the Annamites than she was to the whites. My mother's pupils often came to play with me. I'll never forget their gracefulness, the joy they radiated. They lived in the water—in the rivers and the lakes—when it was hot. And, in fact, the entire landscape of my childhood is a kind of huge watery world.

What other memories do you have of your mother?

She was an extraordinary storyteller. I've forgotten so many things in my life—so many books, so many conversations—but not some of the stories she told us in her drawling voice when she put us to bed at night. The things that most belong to us are, I believe, things that come to us through the direct spoken word.

What do you see in yourself today of your mother?

Her madness left a permanent mark on me. Her pessimism, too. She was constantly expecting war to break out, or a natural catastrophe that would have wiped us all out. She managed to hand on to me this strong, peasant sense of home life—something like a bastion and refuge that she was able to create in each of the houses we lived in.

You've said several times that your mother would rather have had another boy than a daughter and that in your adolescence, you'd have done anything not to disappoint that expectation.

Well, not exactly. She didn't want me to become too educated. That's definitely the case. She had in her such a visceral fear of intellectuals and of everything that might be beyond her. I can't remember seeing her once with a book in her hand. It's for that reason and so many others that I decided to leave for good.

From the banks of the Mekong, what did you imagine life in France was like?

The only image of Europe came from my mother's stories. It wasn't easy for me, when I got there, to adopt Western ways and manners. I suddenly had to wear shoes and eat steak.

• • • THE PARIS YEARS • • •

· · ·

You were just eighteen when you set off alone for Paris.

I realized I'd made a mistake waiting all those years, behind a door, for my family to notice my presence. I wanted to start again, to prove to my mother I could make a go of things. Don't we all run away from home because the only adventure possible is the one our mother has already marked out for us?

In Paris you registered immediately at the university.

I'd been awarded a scholarship. I had to set about doing something. It was very difficult at the start. I began to study mathematics initially, undoubtedly so as to follow in my father's footsteps. [Italo] Calvino and [Raymond] Queneau claim there's a very strong connection between the exact sciences and literature. Then I tried to get into Sciences Po, and in the end I did a law degree. When I took the first exams, I began to get over that endemic sense of wretchedness that my mother had handed on to me—she suffered from an inferiority complex towards people she regarded as important, whether it be colonial civil servants or customs officials.

What sort of life did you lead?

A student life. We went to lectures, met up in the cafes to eat sandwiches and talk, then, in the evening, we went to a brasserie. We were all young and hadn't a penny to our name.

I don't remember much about those years. Perhaps because I never talk about them. They sometimes seem to have been engulfed by darkness.

Who were the first people you got to know in Paris?

Students who, like me, were at the university. Then I met a young Jewish man from Neuilly. I still remember that as one of the most stimulating, crucial encounters of my life. He showed me places and books I knew nothing about, since all I knew were the swamps and the exotic writings of Pierre Loti and Pierre Benoit. He got me to read the Bible and introduced me to music. Every week we went to Mozart, Bach or Haydn concerts.

Did you also go to the opera?

Those were fashionable, middle-class occasions that bored me stiff. I already found opera tedious. Over-spectacular effects that over-face you visually and detract from the contribution of the music. Music—real music—can never be a background to something else. It has to fill us up with—and empty us of—everything.

Do you still listen to music?

> No, to listen to Bach the way I did as a young, naive person, when nothing could shake me, would be painful for me today. We're talking about enormous, harrowing efforts. I want to laugh when people tell me they listened to Mozart *all day long.*

Let's come back to your first years in Paris, the Popular Front years, with the spectacular victory of the Left and the election of Léon Blum, followed by a great many intellectuals becoming politically committed: [André] Gide, [Georges] Bernanos, [André] Malraux, [François] Mauriac.

> I wasn't really politically committed at the time. Politics was something very distant. I felt young and indifferent. For example, the eloquence and commitment of Malraux— even before he became Minister of Culture much later, when I would follow him a little distractedly on television— already seemed just a torrent of rhetoric.

This period without political commitment was a pretty short one for you since a few years later, after your marriage to Robert Antelme—who would later publish a committed work like The Human Race—*and shortly after the declaration of war, you joined the Communist Party. Why?*

> I needed to overcome my loneliness, to leave behind a dias- pora I'd joined enthusiastically and become part of a group, enter into a collective consciousness that could be shared. I knew about the gulags, Stalinism, Siberia, the German–Soviet Pact and the pogroms of 1934, but joining meant recognizing myself in the Party's destiny and

sloughing off my own. At the same time, my misfortune became a class misfortune.

How do you assess your eight years of activism in Communist Party ranks?

I'm still a communist who doesn't recognize herself in communism. To join a party, you have to be more or less autistic, neurotic, deaf and blind. For years, I stayed in the party as a branch secretary, without realizing what was happening, without seeing that the working class was a victim of its own weakness, that even the proletariat was doing nothing to overcome the limitations of its condition.

What caused you, in the late 1950s, to leave the Party?

The Stalinist model spread confusion around revolution, and the events of 1956 in Hungary had sickened me. Obviously, it was traumatic to leave. Only when 1968 happened did I stop feeling like a victim, in spite of myself, of communist ideology. I'd had enough of Marxist demagogy which in its attempt to wipe out individuals' contradictions merely alienated those individuals more. Any attempt to simplify human consciousness has something fascistic about it (in that respect, Stalinism and Hitlerism are the same thing).

What was the view inside the Party of the fact that you were an intellectual and, moreover, that you wrote?

I wrote on the sly in the early years. My comrades didn't even know I had academic qualifications. They lived by very rigid dogmas. Reading and writing books outside the Party's prescribed, ordained texts would have been akin to a theoretical crime that undermined its stifling credo. Anyway, they managed to make me feel guilty—when I began making *Jaune le soleil*, they accused me of anti-communism to stop me going on with it, then they tried to force me to live as part of a couple, a family, like all the other members, as they put it. And there was a scandal when a written report criticized me for going to nightclubs and said that I'd been living with *two* men—my new lover and my former one.

Did the experience of the Communist Party condition your work?

If it had, I wouldn't have been a real writer. When I write I forget all ideology and cultural memory. Only perhaps in *The Sea Wall* is there anything political—in my mother's monologues about poverty and in the description of the colony. But this is still the private dialectic of a desperate woman. I don't believe you write to send messages to readers—you write for yourself, breaking with preceding styles, reinventing them each time.

Do *you* know a Party writer who did that? And don't tell me [Louis] Aragon's surrealism is like that. He wrote well, that's all there is to it. But he didn't change anything and he remained a faithful Party representative who knew how to charm with words.

And yet you believed in a political utopia.

I believed in Allende, in the 1917 revolution, in the Prague Spring, in the early days of Cuba and Che Guevara.

And in 1968? You were a member of the Students and Writers Action Committee.

I believed in it precisely as utopia. Its great strength was to stir up the stagnant waters of Europe—of the whole world, perhaps.

You once said, 'When [Charles] Baudelaire talks about lovers and desire, the revolutionary spirit is strongest in him. When the members of the Central Committee talk about revolution, it's pornography.'[1]

Like all regimes, Marxism is afraid that, if not appropriately channelled, 'certain free forces'—the imagination, poetry, even love—can undermine its foundations, as it were, and it has always set itself up to censor experience, desire.

Among your texts, which do you regard as political?

In *Abahn Sabana David*, there's the whole of my hatred for the Party. David is the symbol of the man anaesthetized by Stalinist demagogy and lies, Abahn is the figure of the intellectual condemned by events to a schizophrenic existence and Sabana is, perhaps, the emblem of pain itself which cannot be concealed. By contrast, in *L'Amour*, there's all my fear of the Apocalypse, the sense of an end of the world. In *Destroy, She Said*, Elisabeth Alione, Alissa and Stein call for the destruction of the world as humanity's only solution.

Alternatively, Destroy could be seen as a kind of manifesto for May 1968.

Madness, as an extreme rejection of models, and utopia, too, save us by distancing and preserving us from everything.

[Michel] Foucault agreed with me on that. I can't understand how [Philippe] Sollers could state that it wasn't a political novel but only a literary one.[2] [Maurice] Blanchot, who knows me very well, understood the revolutionary significance of the text immediately, the love-death pairing, which I pointed to as the only path of salvation, the one, precisely, that involves the total destruction of what existed before and was preventing the unfettered flow of the drives.[3]

What, in your view, was the most useful thing May '68 taught us?

May '68 and the Prague Spring were political failures which profited us much more than any victory, by virtue of the ideological vacuum they created. Not knowing where we were going, as happened to us in the street in those days, but knowing only that we were going, that we were on the move, so to speak, without fear of the consequences and the contradictions—that's what we learnt. But can you be a writer, I wonder, without running up against contradictions? No, at the very best you can be a good storyteller. Clearly, to propose that ideologies be abolished completely isn't easy in a country like France which, from time immemorial, has resisted the idea of any historical period that doesn't bear its own definition within itself. From childhood on, we've been compelled to order our lives, to the point of expunging all disorder from them.

And it's in this fear of the void, in the desire to curb the tiniest risk that might ensue from it, that power roots itself.

Can a Marxist consciousness survive in the current state of things?

I start out from the principle that all political discourses are alike. There's no point in becoming politically committed—Europe is in the grip of sham revolutions and Marxism is now a conceptual, cerebral and, as such, corpse-like doctrine.

The heroine of one of your political texts, Le Camion [The Lorry], *says: 'Let the world go hang, let it go hang, that's the only policy.'*[4]

I no longer believe in anything and not believing can perhaps lead to that '[creative] act against all power', the only possible response to the oligarchy of the banks and the false democracy that governs us.

But at the last elections you voted Socialist all the same.

A sort of non-vote indicating the desire to find a solution between two oppressors. And I say that despite the great esteem in which I hold my friend [François] Mitterand. Yet, after the Communist Party I'll never be able to commit myself to a political party line again.

You and François Mitterand have known each other for many years.

Yes, since Resistance days. He's one of the rare—and one of the first—people I send all my books to. I'm sure he'll read them and call me to talk about them together. He's a man who loves life very much, Mitterand. Of course, as long as he's president, he won't be able to say all that he thinks about the Communist Party and about today's France.

Whenever I've seen [Jacques] Chirac and him on television in recent years, the difference between them has been striking. The one is open, ready to accept change and dialogue, the other is hidebound by an outdated language, the defender of an egocentric nation and a society closed in exclusively on itself and fearful of everything from outside, whether it be intellectuals, Jews, Arabs, Chinese, Argentinians, Palestinians...

The transcript of some of these interviews and encounters between the president and yourself on topical matters was published in L'Autre Journal *a few years back.[5]*

He enjoyed these discussions and even pressed me to carry on with them. We spoke, most often at my home, then I transcribed the discussions, he corrected them, I corrected them again and he let me have my way. We would howl with laughter...

With regard to journalism, from the late 1950s onwards you took an active part in the political and social life of your country, commenting on various subjects in the pages of weekly or daily publications, from Le Monde, France-Observateur *(later* Le Nouvel Observateur) *and even women's magazines such as* Vogue *or* Sorcières, *to your more recent writing in* Libération *and in* L'Autre Journal.

It's something I've always liked, the urgency of journalistic writing. The text has to have in it the force—and why not, also, the limitations—of the haste in which it was written. Before being consumed and thrown away.

After begging me to comment on some event or other, the editors of *Le Monde* often didn't actually have the courage to publish my article . . .

As for *L'Autre Journal*, which is one of the left-wing literary magazines I like best, they said that if I wrote for them, it would push up sales.

What were your reasons for taking up this journalistic career?

I suddenly found it necessary to set out publicly what I thought about certain subjects. It was a need to come out into the open, to see what I was capable of outside the four walls of my room. I began to write articles in my empty moments, during the pauses in my daily writing. When I was writing a book, I didn't even read the newspapers. But the articles took me a lot of time—you can't imagine how long. I felt a great deal of pressure, even though I'd been doing it for years.

What should the function of journalism be?

To create public opinion around events that would otherwise pass unnoticed.

I don't think there can be professional objectivity: I prefer a clear position to be taken. A sort of moral stance. Something writers can very well do without in their own books.

You've always had—and still have—a passionate interest in certain news stories. Often your positions—taken up on TV or in the daily papers— don't go down well with public opinion.

The temptation to say what I was thinking—to denounce the social injustice of French people's reluctance to reflect on the Algerian war, on the rise of totalitarian regimes, on the militarization of the planet and a forced moralization of society—that's something I've always felt.

What interested me most was the impact all that had on individuals in terms of the madness or randomness within them, their harbouring of crimes of passion or of desperation. Or simply my interest in certain aspects of human beings which the legal system feels it can treat like any other, as something irreversible, as natural events.

Four years ago, in a long article in Libération,[6] you turned your attention to the case of Christine Villemin, who was presumed to have murdered her son in a village in the Vosges. You told how you yourself went to Lépanges-sur-Vologne and, without having been present at the crime, you were able to imagine the exact course of events; taking on the totality of the case—without too much verisimilitude perhaps—to the point where you made Christine Villemin a 'necessarily sublime' heroine. The very emblem of writing as an irreversible and total process, insofar as it is driven by obscure alien forces. The woman's crazed act could therefore be said to have been, as you saw it, the ultimate attempt (hence innocent and not blameworthy) to find herself and free herself, with her destiny, through the murder of an unwanted child.

Christine Villemin's crime is the offence of someone who was above all, like every woman, a victim—reduced to the materiality of existence, incapable of surmounting that condition, condemned to live out a hollow, unwanted life.[7]

Your unconditional defence of Christine Villemin caused a scandal: many intellectuals and showbiz personalities, including Simone Signoret, joined forces against you.

> Christine Villemin was the prototype of a femininity subjugated by men, it being men who lay down the laws of the couple, of sex and desire. There are women like her everywhere, incapable of expressing themselves and exhausted by the emptiness that surrounds them—children are nothing but a further shackle on their self-realization.[8]

Anyway, your reportage would include journeys to the fringes of society—ghettos, prisons, the street or, by contrast, convents—to meet prisoners, murderers, Carmelites, proletarians, Africans, Jews.

> What I wanted to do was to give a voice to people we simply knew nothing about in the economic boom years. To lend such impact to certain kinds of testimony—a harrowing case of self-defence by an Algerian worker, the horrendous intellectual emptiness of the life of a Carmelite nun—that they could no longer be ignored by the bourgeois class or used by them for their own ends.

What image do you have of the future and of human progress?

> Robotization, telecommunications and computerization are relieving humanity of the need for exertion but ultimately blunting its creative capacities. The danger is that we'll see a one-dimensional man, a humanity without memory. But to talk of the problems of humanity means nothing—the constant battle, day after day, is the battle one fights with oneself in the attempt to resolve the

unsolved problem of oneself. Or in finding oneself, as ever, up against the problem of God.

Do you believe in God?

To know that, if there's a divinity, it can only be within us, seeing that there's only emptiness around us, is no help in solving the problem. Not believing in God is just one more credo. I doubt whether it's possible not to believe at all. That would be like removing all meaning, all eternity from the great passions of our lives. Everything would become an end in itself, with no consequences. Though we can't rule out the future of humanity being just that, either.

Can we, in your view, speak of human happiness?

That's a word—happiness—we should never pronounce. The very meaning we give to the word would be warped, so to speak, and its scope would be exceeded—it's inaccessible, extraordinarily mysterious.

Do you believe in chance?

I like feeling myself part of the great game of life, incapable of controlling or foreseeing how things will work out. I think the general unease people feel comes from that, from the tragic consciousness that they aren't in control of the outcome of their own lives to the extent that they'd like.

Does the idea of death frighten you?

I realized that it did the last time I was in hospital.[9] I was told that if I had another drink, it would kill me. At that point I was gripped by a strange fear, the fear of a hunted animal.

As a youngster, for more than thirty years, I feared madness more than death. I was always being told I was mad or illogical. But inside me was merely a semblance of disorder or contradictoriness. In the end, they induced a minor neurosis in me and I had to make great efforts to free myself from this sense of madness that men managed to conjure up in me.

There's a lot of talk, on this threshold of the third millennium, of the end of the world.

The fear of the year 2000 and of the end of the world is fanciful. Everyone's saying it's to be expected, but no one's saying why. By comparison with the mystical anxiety surrounding the Apocalypse of the year 1000, our fear is a cool one, a fear empirically aware of the danger of irreversible decline. There's no longer any idea of a 'sacred' death behind this, as in the past, but, at best, the idea of nothingness.

Episodes like the explosion of the nuclear power station at Chernobyl[10] testify to the reality of a gradually advancing collective end to humanity, as yet incalculable in its scope. Everyone should have decided to shut their nuclear power stations down, but no one's done it. The countries of the Third World will always need to have them operating. And then, what would be the point of shutting down the power stations if they would still be dangerous even when closed? The nuclear zones will never be turned back into cornfields.

• • • TRAJECTORIES OF WRITING • • •

. . .

For what reasons did you choose to write?

> The need to put on the blank page something I felt to be urgent without having the strength to do it completely. I was reading a lot at that time and, inevitably, I was in such a hurry to write that I wasn't always aware of all the influences on me. It's only with the second book that you begin to have insight into where your writing is going, through slow detachment from the fascination that the *idea* of literature exerts on us.

How did you begin?

> At eleven I was living in Cochinchina, where it was thirty degrees in the shade every day. I wrote poems—that's where it always begins—about the world and life, which I knew nothing about.

Your first book, Les Impudents, *dates from 1943. You were twenty-nine years old.*

> It was about the hatred I felt for my elder brother. I sent the manuscript to Queneau—I didn't know him—who was

working at Gallimard. I was nervous when I walked into his office, but sure of myself. The book had already been rejected by all the other publishers, but I was sure that this time it would be accepted. Queneau didn't say it was good. He simply looked up and said, 'Madame, you are a writer.' The next year he published *La Vie tranquille*. It was so badly constructed, so insistent and naive in its realism.

Up to *Moderato Cantabile*, it was as though I didn't recognize the books I wrote. *The Sea Wall* or *The Little Horses of Tarquinia* are still books that are too *full*, books in which everything—too much—is *said*. Nothing's left to the reader's imagination. There may be some connection with what I now regard as my mature phase. At a pinch, I can see one with some aspects of *The Sailor from Gibraltar*: a woman is caught up in an endless wait for a sailor, an inaccessible love. It's something very similar to what I'm writing at the moment.

For years I had a social life, and the ease with which I met people or spoke to them was reflected in my books. Up to the point where I had relations with a man and gradually all that worldly-mindedness disappeared. That was a violent, highly erotic love affair, and, for the first time, I felt it was beyond my control. It even made me want to kill myself and that changed the very way I produced literature—it was now about discovering the gaps, the blanks I had within me, and finding the courage to express them. The woman in *Moderato Cantabile* and the one in

Hiroshima mon amour were me. Exhausted by that passion and unable to talk about it, I decided to write about it, almost coldly.

In 1950 came The Sea Wall, *the real book about your adolescence.*

And also the most popular, the easiest. Five thousand copies sold. Queneau showed a child-like enthusiasm for the book. He did a great deal of promotion and I came very close to winning the Prix Goncourt. But it was a political, anti-colonialist book and in those days they didn't give prizes to communists. I got it thirty-four years later for *The Lover*, which takes up the same themes as it happens: a life of poverty in the colonies, sex, money, a lover, a mother and brothers.

What did you feel writing The Lover?

A certain happiness. The book had obscure origins—it had come out of the obscurity to which I'd consigned my childhood—and it lacked order. A series of unconnected episodes which I found and abandoned without lingering over them. Episodes I didn't flag up in advance or bring to a conclusion.

What induced you to tell this story which you refer to yourself as inexpressible?

The illness and tiredness I was recovering from had left me with a desire to get back to being myself again after such a long time. I see it as the product not so much of inspiration as of a feel for writing. *The Lover* is a wild text, and it was

Yann Andréa with his book *M. D.* who showed me this savage side I have in me.[1]

Are there characters and situations in the novel that are taken from reality?

I'd had to lie for years about so many stories from the past. My mother was still alive and there were some things I didn't want her to know. And then one day I was alone and I said to myself, why not tell the truth now? Everything in the book is true: the clothes, my mother's anger, the sickly sweet food she made us eat, the Chinese lover's limousine.

Even the money he gave you?

I felt it was my duty to take it from a millionaire and give it to the household. He gave me presents, dragging us around in his car and inviting us all to the dearest restaurant in Saigon. When we were eating, no one spoke a word to him; they were a bit racist in the colonies and my family said they hated him. Of course, when it came to money, they turned a blind eye. At least we wouldn't have to sell or pawn the furniture in order to eat.

What other memories do you have of the man?

I didn't like his Chinese body, but he knew how to pleasure mine. And that was the thing I discovered with him—only then.

The force of desire?

Yes, total. Beyond feelings, impersonal, blind. It was inexpressible. Where that man was concerned, I loved his love of me and that eroticism, inflamed on each occasion by our deep ambiguity.

You sold a million and a half copies of The Lover *in France alone. It's been translated into twenty-six languages. How do you explain this enormous success?*

To think that Jérôme Lindon, my publisher, had only printed five thousand! It was out of print within a few days. Within a month, the print-run had gone up to twenty thousand and I gave the book no further thought. I didn't open it again—that's what I always do. Love, I'm told, is a subject that guarantees success. But that wasn't what I was thinking about as I was writing it. In fact, I was more or less certain I'd bore my readers or irritate them with themes I'd actually covered already. Obviously, I hadn't foreseen that, in coming along with me in these pages, people were going to make it a sort of popular novel.

What might the other ingredients have been that brought such resounding success?

I believe the book conveys the enormous pleasure which I felt for ten hours a day as I was writing it. Normally French literature mistakes tedium in a book for seriousness. And indeed, if people don't finish the books they read, that's because the books are highly pretentious—stupidly pretentious in wanting to refer on to something beyond ...

Do you realize that you're now known throughout the world for having written The Lover—*and sometimes only for that?*

At last no one can say now that Duras writes 'intellectual stuff' . . .

Would you like to point to some particular key to the interpretation of The Lover?

It's a novel and that's all there is to it. Which doesn't lead or go anywhere. The story doesn't conclude, it's just the book that ends. Love and sexual pleasure aren't 'stories' and the other—deeper—reading, if it exists, isn't immediately evident. Everyone can choose to glimpse it.

What, as you see it, have been the most radical changes to your style from the time of The Lover *onwards?*

None. My writing is the same as it's always been. In that, at least, I can give myself free rein without fear. People now are no longer afraid of what, in appearance at least, seems incoherent.

Since The Lover, *your writing has become more and more rarefied.*

It's the sound of the words that's changed from what it was before—like something that might be said to have acquired a kind of involuntary simplicity.

Explain that more.

The Lover is a book so full of literature that it seems, paradoxically, very far removed from it. You don't see—you aren't supposed to see—the artifice, that's all.

You're stubbornly determined not to speak of 'style' with regard to that novel.

It's a 'physical' style, if we must talk about that. *The Lover* came out of a series of photographs that I rediscovered by chance and I began it with the idea of subordinating the text to the images. But the writing gained the upper hand, it ran out of my control, and it was only when I reread it that I noticed how it was built on metonyms. There are words like 'desert', 'white' and 'pleasure' that stand out and connote the whole of the narrative.

To take another of your successes, what do you think is the strength of a book like The War: A Memoir?

The fact that I chose, as point of view, the state of fear of a woman who has to speak about war, and not just general themes. That some tiny facts are recounted, even relating to human physiology in its most animal aspects, such as the shrivelled body of my husband when he got back from Dachau or the story of the Gestapo man Pierre Rabier who wanted to sleep with me, a story I exploited to the full, so as to be able to show his guilt. Or the even more atrocious story of the interrogation I inflicted on the man who was informing on us to the Germans.

The War: A Memoir is a brave text, a mix of the horrific and the sacred, one of the most important I've written. The writing is harsh, it's modern in the sense that it narrates all the events with precision. I'm told it reminds people of [Georges] Bataille. But I'll say again that it isn't literature. It's something more and something less.

Did you really get the material for the book from notebooks you kept during the war, which turned up miraculously in a cupboard?

A lot of critics in France didn't believe me. I can show them my diaries if they like. I can't remember at what date I began them. I only know we're talking about drafts, fragments, notes about novels I was planning at the time—*The Sailor* [from Gibraltar], *The Sea Wall*. And then, you see, you can lie about lots of things, but not about that, not about the actual substance of pain.

To come to one of your more recent publications, between the lines you claim that a book like Blue Eyes, Black Hair—*a story of the impossible passion between a woman and a homosexual man—is autobiographical in its content, though in fact it reproduces the kernel of one of your other stories,* The Malady of Death.

A real-life story, yes. And from not so very long ago, if that's what you want to know . . . Peter Handke and Luc Bondy had asked me to adapt *The Malady of Death* for the Schaubühne in Berlin. Two days after I'd sent it to them, I called to ask them to send it back. In writing the text for the stage, I realized I'd fallen into all the traps I'd been trying to avoid. In other words, I'd given a 'constructed' form to a text which shouldn't have had one, which will never be 'finished', and that it was from precisely this incompletion that it derived its strength. I felt as though I was the victim of an enforced formal failing and I rewrote the adaptation three times without finding a solution. I spoke about it with Yann, I told him I couldn't write any more. Knowing my way of working—crises, second thoughts, revisions—he didn't believe me. And then one evening in June—it was in 1986 at Trouville—I began to write just like that, about the heat, about the summer evenings. And the story came.

Yann Andréa was involved in reading the text?

He was going through a great crisis. He was driving round trying to pick up men for up to ten hours a day. When he stopped, he wept and blamed me. He seemed to want to scream something at me that he couldn't explain, even to himself. Then he went out again. I never knew where he was going. To nightclubs, I suppose, in search of men, to bars, to the lobbies of the big hotels, all dressed in white. While I was writing the story of a woman in love with a man who, without wishing to, detests his own desire.

In 1985, Peter Handke filmed the story.

On my advice and following Blanchot's assessment, he re-worked the text. Indeed, he made it his own. The film is much, much more romantic than the way I'd presented the story. The true malady of death, for Handke, between man and woman is simply the lack of feeling.

In The Unavowable Community,[2] *Blanchot speaks at great length of* The Malady of Death. *On the subject of passion, he writes: 'The latter pledges us fatally and, as if in spite of ourselves, to another who attracts us all the more in that he seems beyond the possibility of ever being* rejoined, being so far beyond everything that matters to us.' And, further on, he writes: 'Assuredly, as time passes, and his realization that with her time no longer passes, and that thus he is deprived of his small properties, "his own room," which being inhabited seems empty—and it is the emptiness she sets up which makes it clear that she is supernumerary—as time passes he happens upon the thought that she ought to disappear and that everything would be easier if she returned to the sea (from which he believes her to have come), a thought that does not reach beyond the stray impulse to think . . . But he makes the mistake of talking to others about it or even of laughing about it, as if that attempt made with utmost seriousness, ready to give his whole life to it, left in his memory but the derisiveness of the illusory. And this is exactly one of the traits of the community, when that community dissolves itself, giving the impression of never having been able to exist, even when it did exist.' We would like to take, to steal in contravention of all laws. And to steal something which will, in reality, always be beyond our grasp. The accomplishment of all love is achieved only through the loss of what, in reality, we never had: it is precisely the alterity between man and woman that creates this 'eternally provisional and always already deserted community'. It is indeed 'unavowable': like all communities, that of lovers will never be able to speak itself or give itself; and, in dissipating itself, it will leave the trace of something which, while already having taken place, has never existed.

Yes, that's it exactly.

What prompted you to publish Practicalities, *that faithful transcription of autobiographical interviews—or, rather, of certain associations of ideas from your memory—that you granted to Jérôme Beaujour?*

Wanting to be able to say things that I think but have never written at any time in my life, things that have gladdened or troubled me and which no one in the general run of my interviews has ever asked me about.

There was talk not so long ago, with regard to [Alain] Robbe-Grillet and the last book of his memoirs, Angélique ou l'enchantement *[Angélique, or Enchantment], of the 'new autobiography', the way we talk of the 'New Novel'. Claiming inspiration from [Marcel] Proust's* Contre Sainte-Beuve *[Against Sainte-Beuve] and repeatedly citing the case of* The Lover, *Robbe-Grillet adopted that expression to refer to new styles of autobiographical writing based not so much on stable or coherent facts of memory as on these series of 'shifting, floating fragments in the text that might be said, precisely, to render the instability and unreliability of memory.'*

Look at a text like *Savannah Bay:* An old woman on the stage who is reliving a confused past, of which only the image of a scorching, white rock remains. A past that mingles with the present, so unreal that it may have been transfigured—or even invented.

And your last novel, Emily L, *also had a difficult gestation.*

Indeed, it did! And yet there's something diabolical in me that enabled me, at times, to write a book in a week... The same ease with which I wrote essays when I was at school.

I sometimes feel as though *Emily L* wasn't written by me. That I simply looked on as it was being written. It was Irène Lindon, Jérôme's daughter,[3] who insisted I finish it.

She came round to my flat almost every day to pick up the pages. She had them typed up and brought them back to me for correction.

You've said yourself that the book was like The Ravishing of Lol V. Stein *in some respects.*

The difference is that in this case, there's a woman observing another woman's story without being directly involved in it—unlike what happens with Lola Valérie Stein, nothing of what happens here is influenced by the reality of the other woman, Emily, sitting in the cafe.

The Ravishing of Lol V. Stein *is regarded as your most complex novel— both from the stylistic viewpoint and because of some of its thematic implications. Lacan himself devoted some pages to you in his seminars.*

I was in rehab when I wrote it. And I'll always associate the book with the fear of living without alcohol.

The Ravishing is a novel in itself, the story of a woman driven mad by a latent love that never declares itself, that's never played out. In other words, from the moment at the S. Thala ball when Lol sees her fiancé Michael Richardson leave with another woman, Anne-Marie Stretter, her whole life will unfold around that very loss, that very void. Lol is a prisoner, mad with an existence she can't manage to live.

The void you just alluded to is that 'lack' which Lacan sees as the origin and end of all existence.[4] The lack of an order, of a centre where the— irremediably disconnected—self could find itself.

It's true, all my books are born and move around just such a point that's always evoked yet always missing.

It's exactly that. A character who doesn't speak and isn't there (Anne-Marie Stretter, the Chinese lover, the sailor from Gibraltar, the woman in *The Malady of Death*) or an event that doesn't occur (as in *The Square*, *Le Navire Night*, *Moderato Cantabile*, *The Little Horses of Tarquinia*) are what trigger the story. The longing for a story.

To come back to The Ravishing . . . , *what sort of relationship did you have with Lacan?*

He talked about Freud right away. About the period in which he was arguing that artists are always ahead of analysts in the pursuit and analysis of the object. I tried to explain to him that I was unaware myself how Lol came about.

He thought highly of me, no doubt, with that attitude typical of men—and even more of male intellectuals—that's judgemental about women.

As for me, I don't read him. Quite honestly I can't understand much of what he wrote.

Did you meet often?

We met up one evening, I remember, in a cafe in central Paris. He fired questions at me for two hours. I barely got an answer in. I couldn't always follow him. Lol, he said, was the classical example of a clinical delirium—the drama of evoking the primal scene between the two parents and the child—because he was convinced the key to everything was to be found in this name which he believed I'd devised wittingly for the little madwoman: Lol V. Stein. That is to say—and here I decode—'wings of paper', plus the V that indicated 'scissors' (in deaf-and-dumb language) and Stein, which meant 'stone'. Scissors, paper, stone in French is *le jeu de la mourre*, which led him to the direct association with *le jeu de l'amour*—the game of love. You are, he added, a 'ravisher' and we readers are the 'ravished'.[5]

Do you believe in psychoanalysis?

Freud's a great writer, a facile writer if you like. As for Freudianism, it's an embalmed, self-absorbed discipline. It employs a language that's at odds with the normal code, with a diminishing purchase on the outside world. All in all, psychoanalysis doesn't interest me much. I don't believe I need it—perhaps also because I write. But I don't think it's enough for the mental patient to be aware of his own neurosis to be cured of it.

Since 1943, you've published fifteen novels, not to mention the plays and screenplays.[6] What do you feel each time a book is about to come out?

Until it sees the light of day, a book is something shapeless that's afraid of being born, of coming out. Like a creature you carry within yourself, it demands fatigue, silence, solitude and slowness. But once it's out, that will all disappear in a flash.

To become what?

Something that belongs to everyone, to all those who, taking it in hand, wish to make it their own. You have to free the book from the cage of writing, give it life, make it capable of circulating, of allowing people to dream. They tell me *Hiroshima mon amour* has inspired a song.

Yes, it's an English group, Ultravox, who sing it.[7]

I'm pleased about that. I like people to take my things for their own.

For L'Amour, *you've changed publisher in Italy. You're not with your usual publishers (Feltrinelli and Einaudi) but with Mondadori.*

I'm always happy when someone pays me more.

The title isn't original.

I decided on it after I'd finished the book, as a reaction against all the books with that same title. It isn't a story about love, but about everything in passion that remains suspended and incapable of being named. The entire meaning of the book lies there, in that ellipsis.

Speaking of writing, Graham Greene says every writer, sooner or later, falls victim to a real 'writer's block'. Can you remember any moments of that kind?

I've already spoken about the crisis I experienced over the adaptation of *The Malady of Death*. Before 1968, as it happens, I wrote regularly every day, sitting at this table, exactly like going to an office. Then, suddenly, at that point came a crisis. For almost a year my imagination was blocked.

And then, finally, *Destroy, She Said* arrived like a bolt from the blue. I didn't spend more than five or six days working on it. Since then, it's always been like that—the books come out after long, infinitely long silences.

• • • TOWARDS A TEXTUAL ANALYSIS • • •

. . .

The suspension of syntactic underpinnings, the abolition of a certain
expressive linearity and the triumph of narrative analysis impart a sense
of the unsayable to your text.

The empty spaces between one fragment and another—what you call
'typographic blanks' (similar, in fact, to the black screens that punctuate
some of your films)—and then the silences which follow the dialogue,
both on the page and on film, and the intermittent nature of the discourse
detach speech itself from its habitual context, creating a new semantics.

It's a break in the automatic mechanisms of language, a
cleansing of the wear that time inflicts on it.

Being no longer imprisoned or saturated by the structure of the narration,
the reader's imaginary, his desire, what you call his 'nostalgia for fiction',
will be freed up—not so much by an exaggerated accumulation of details
as by their very absence.

It's only out of what is missing, out of the blank spaces that
appear in a sequence of significations—out of the gaps—
that something can be born.

It is silence, exactly. Discretion in both dialogue and love affairs—what is left unsaid or merely alluded to—takes up a large part of your work. The only activity that identifies your characters seems to be the activity of speech.

They speak as though they are giving up definitively on life, attempting to find ersatz solutions for the inconstancy of existence. Take the woman in Le Camion—*when the lorry driver asks her what she normally talks about with the people she meets, she merely answers, 'I talk.' As if to say that it's precisely the things one speaks about that have now lost their importance. With the man and the girl in* The Square, *the lovers of* Hiroshima *or of* The Malady of Death *or* La Musica, Navire Night *and* Moderato Cantabile, *all they have left is speech, which is needed, we might say, by all the world's lovers as a very confirmation of their 'being-there', as a last crutch of incommunicability. However, discourse is internally self-defeating, given the intrinsic impossibility of getting through to the other person. In stubbornly going on speaking, we might say, your characters just go on lying to themselves. As if in imitation of the rhythms and rites of a sacred, metaphysical ceremonial, their dialogues, like the refrain of a song, possess a hieratic rhythm that comes from the sentences themselves. The flow of speech is interrupted by a great many silences: the value of these—and what they communicate—is greater than the value of any words.*

Do you remember *The Princesse de Clèves?*[1] In that book the silences of the princess and the Duke of Nemours might genuinely be called silences of love. The words that will never pass between them are merely a spurious, inadequate means of expressing desire. But the ambiguity of that silence amplifies and suspends every moment of passion. It's the same with Robert Musil. A book like *The Man Without Qualities* could only ever remain unfinished.

Look at the relationship between the brother and sister, in which sex, though spoken about, never materializes: as though it were only like that—on the threshold of the sayable—that literature could be produced.

Could you define the narrative techniques you use?

Everything starts from the spoken word. The meaning of the language I use doesn't concern me as I'm writing. If it has a meaning, that will unfurl within the text, as it does in Baudelaire's poetry.

With The Lover, *you spoke about a 'flowing writing'.*[2]

That's this way of showing things on the page, moving from one to the other without emphasis or explanation, from the description of my brother to describing the tropical forest, from the depth of desire to the deep blue of the sky.

Memory, digressions and flashbacks have always been an integral part of the narrative structure of your works.

It's often thought that life is punctuated chronologically by events. In reality, we don't know their significance. It's memory that restores their lost meaning to us. And yet all that remains visible and expressible is often the superfluous, the mere appearances, the surface of our experience. The rest stays inside, obscure, so intense that we can't even speak of it. The more intense things are, the more difficult it becomes for them to surface in their entirety. Working with memory in the classical sense doesn't interest me—it's not about stores of memory that we can dip into for facts, as we like. Moreover, the very act of forgetting is necessary—absolutely. If eighty per cent of what happened to us wasn't repressed, then living would be unbearable. True memory is forgetting, emptiness—the memory that enables us not to succumb to the oppression of recollection and of the blinding pain which, fortunately, we have forgotten.

Citing Flaubert, and with him a large part of the contemporary literary tradition, Jacqueline Risset has spoken of your work as an uninterrupted series of 'books about nothing'.[3] Novels built precisely on nothingness.

To write isn't to tell a story, but to evoke what there is around it; you create around the story, one moment after another. Everything there is, but everything which might also not be or which might be interchangeable—like the events of life. The story and its unreality, or its absence.

Is that how you explain your recurrent, unusual use of the conditional?

The conditional is better than any other mode at rendering the idea of artificiality that underlies both literature and cinema. Each event appears as the potential, hypothetical consequence of something else. When they're playing, being thoroughly conscious of the fiction and, at the same time, of the frivolity of play, children are constantly using verbs in the conditional tense.

Often—I'm thinking of examples like Suzanne Andler *and* The Square— *instead of coming to a conclusion, your novels end on the adverb 'perhaps', connoting the random character of their endings.*

I've always distrusted stories that suddenly 'end'.

Your non-stories might be said to resort to a sort of zero degree of the novelistic imaginary. And yet you simply maintain a single discourse, which is both epic and already somewhat hackneyed—the discourse of love.

Only a certain idiotic avant-garde believed they could renew literature by racking their brains to explore unknown places.

Rather than employing recondite, refined formulations, the language you use seems to draw on a certain vigorous everyday speech.

An automatic process of paring and shrinking down the raw material of language goes on inside me. An aspiration to stylistic economy, to a geometric space where every word stands bare.

In your most recent novels, Blue Eyes, Black Hair *and* Emily L. *(and even more so in your films thanks to the use of voice-overs) you use the technique called 'double narration'. The narrator is someone who, while being involved in the story in the first person, is watching another story that's unfolding simultaneously. Hence, the point of view is offset or split off from the core narrative.*

What reaches the reader is never the direct story, the plain account of what happened. At the very most it is the emotion, the sublimated residue. Isn't that how it is when we tell our dreams?

The gaze, the endless intersection of gazes melting into one another, remains the true cognitive instrument to which the reality of characters and history unveils itself. Gazes superimposed on one another. Each character looks at someone, and is looked at by someone, who in turn is observed by someone else. All without it being possible for the whole to be reduced to the supreme, omniscient gaze—that of the narrator in this case—who would encapsulate and express them all. The plot of Lol V. Stein is highly representative: a real story of voyeurism. The heroine shows a particular interest in the course of the other events. Just as, at the beginning of the narrative, Lol had been present when her fiancé Michael Richardson had met Anne-Marie Stretter, so, subsequently, in the unconscious desire endlessly to perpetuate the scene of the two lovers, who more or less relegate her to the role of eternal spectator, she is present at the meeting between Jacques Hold and Tatiana Karl.

Voyeurism—there are numerous examples, from certain triangles in L'Amour *to what happens in* Destroy, She Said, Moderato Cantabile *and* Emily L.*—is a constant theme of your work. As if in a desire to confirm the hypothesis of the continuous presence of a third party watching passion arise within a couple.*

I've always thought that love was a three-cornered affair—one eye watching on while desire circulates from one person to the other. Psychoanalysis speaks of a compulsive repetition of the primal scene. Personally, I would speak of writing as the third element of a story. And, indeed, we never coincide entirely with what we do; we are never entirely where we believe we are. There is a gap between ourselves and our actions, and everything happens *outside*. Characters look, knowing they are themselves being looked at. They are excluded and, at the same time, included in the 'primal scene' which unfolds before them once again.

Your films and novels don't obey linearity or succession in the temporal dimension. Just as the unity of time has disintegrated—which through flashbacks and foretastes of what will be narrated later turns cyclically on itself—so the unities of place and action collapse too.

The criterion you follow is that of simultaneity—not one, but three actions at once are taken apart and reassembled in parallel, compressed montages.

Corresponding with each event is something happening elsewhere. The time of the story coincides, then, with the immediate restoration of an inner time for the individual characters and the—liberated—flow of an action in terms of various spatiotemporal coordinates.

The events of our lives are never unique, nor do they succeed one another unambiguously, as we would wish. Multiple and irreducible, they echo infinitely in consciousness; they come and go from our past to the future, spreading like an echo, like circles rippling out in water, constantly exchanging places.

• • • LITERATURE • • •

• • •

Why, as you see it, do people begin to write?

I have in mind here my last novel, *Emily L.* Emily reads, she writes poems. Everything, in fact, began with literature, as suggested to her by her father; everything begins with some poems by Emily Dickinson that are the—distant—inspiration for the book. I don't really know what pushes people to write except, perhaps, a lonely childhood. For me, as for Emily, there was a father or a book or a teacher or a woman lost in the paddy fields of Cochinchina. Do you know what, I don't think I've ever got to know anyone without asking myself this question: When people don't write, what do they do? I have a secret admiration for people who don't and yet, as a matter of fact, I don't know how they're able not to.

What relation is there between writing and the real?

All writers, whether they wish to or not, are talking about themselves. About themselves and the main event in their lives. In the very places where we seem to be telling of things alien to ourselves, it's ourselves and our obsessions that are in play. It's the same with dreams, as Freud says—it's simply our egoism showing through.

The writer has two lives: one, on the surface of the self, which makes him talk and act day by day. And the other, the real life, which follows him everywhere and gives him no rest.

To what extent is the autobiographical element important to you?

The beginnings of a story you write always lie with *others*, with the people you meet, love and observe closely. It's stupid to think, as some writers do—even great ones—that we're alone in the world.

In With Open Eyes: Conversations with Matthieu Galey, *Marguerite Yourcenar claims 'When I write I am carrying out a task, writing under my own dictation, as it were. I am performing the difficult and exhausting labour of putting my own thought in order, straightening out my own dictation.'[1]*

One fragment after the other, little by little, without trying to find direct correspondences between the different periods—I let the connections form unwittingly.

Writing, consequently, as passive gestation, the revelation of something one already knows...

It's about deciphering what exists within us already in a rudimentary state, indecipherable to others, in what I call the 'site of passion'.

Could you define the actual process of your writing?

It's an incorrigible inspiration that comes to me more or less once a week, then disappears for months. A very ancient injunction—the need to sit oneself down to write without as yet knowing what. The writing itself attests to this ignorance, to this search for the shadowy place where the entirety of experience is gathered.

For a long time I thought writing was a job of work. I'm now convinced that it's an inner event, a 'non-work' that you accomplish, above all, by emptying yourself out, and allowing what's already *self-evident* to percolate through. I wouldn't speak so much about economy, form or composition of prose as about balances of opposing forces that have to be identified, classified, contained by language. Like a musical score. If you don't take that into account, then you do indeed write 'free' books, but writing has nothing to do with that kind of freedom.

So that would be the ultimate reason you write?

What's painful is having to *perforate* our inner darkness until its primal potency spreads over the whole page, converting what is by nature 'internal' into something 'external'. That's why I say that only the mad write absolutely. Their memory is a 'holed' memory, addressed totally to the outside world.

Writing to exorcize one's fantasies? You yourself argue that writing is therapeutic.

As a child, I was always afraid of contamination by leprosy. It's only afterwards, writing about it somewhere, that leprosy lost its terror for me, if that can explain things for you.

I write to be coarsened, to be torn to pieces, and then to lose my importance, to unburden myself—for the text to take my place so that I exist less. There are only two ways I manage to free myself of me: by the idea of suicide and the idea of writing.

Yourcenar claims that a writer 'is useful if he clarifies the reader's thinking, rids him of timidity or prejudice, or makes him see and feel things that he would not otherwise have seen or felt'.[2]

Yes, real writers are necessary. They give form to what others feel in a shapeless way—that's why totalitarian regimes banish them.

What, as you see it, is the task of literature?

To represent what's forbidden. To say what isn't normally said. Literature *must* be scandalous—all the activities of the mind today must have some risk and adventure in them. The poet himself embodies this very risk, as someone who, unlike us, doesn't put up defences against life.

Look at [Arthur] Rimbaud, [Paul] Verlaine . . . But Verlaine only comes afterwards. The greatest is still Baudelaire—it took him just twenty poems to achieve eternity.

You alluded in an interview to precise features that might be said to distinguish masculine writing from feminine.

There's a close, natural relation that has always linked women with silence and, hence, with knowledge of themselves, with self-awareness. That leads their writing towards that authenticity which male writing lacks, its structure relating too greatly to bodies of ideological or theoretical knowledge.

In short, men can be said to be more connected to knowledge, understood as cultural baggage?

And hence to power, to authority, which are not in themselves related to *genuine* writing. Look at what Roland Barthes has written on love. Fascinating fragments—meticulous, intelligent and literary, but cold. The words of someone who knows love only by reading about it or seeing it from afar, without knowing its transports, its impulses, its pain. There's nothing in what he writes that isn't extremely controlled. It was only thanks to his homosexuality that Proust was able, by being thrust into the twists and turns of passion, to make literature out of it at the same time.

Don't you think you're going a bit far there?

By masculine writing, I mean writing that's too weighed down with ideas. Proust, Stendhal, [Herman] Melville and Rousseau have no sex.

Talking of your relations with Raymond Queneau, you've told how you quarrelled with him over a judgement he'd passed on your book The Square, *criticizing it for its excessive romanticism, when you'd wanted to leave a highly materialistic imprint on it.*

On that occasion, he really didn't get it. Any more than those who read the book only as a love story . . .

What other memories do you have of Queneau and your meetings with him?

> I liked him. I think *Zazie in the Metro*'s an extraordinary book. But I ask myself this: Who knows how Queneau would have ended up if he hadn't been afraid of himself, of the deep recesses of his thinking?

Did you talk about writing in those days when you had dealings with him?

> He had his own way of going through the manuscripts that came in to Gallimard. He claimed it only took a few pages to form an idea of them—not so much to know if the book was well executed or not, but whether the author was an egocentric amateur splurging across the page like a girl writing her diary, or whether you were dealing with a genuine—if not necessarily good—writer. The writer, he used to tell me, is someone who realizes they're not alone as they confront the text.

What relations did you have with the authors of the Nouveau Roman—Nathalie Sarraute, Alain Robbe-Grillet, Claude Ollier, Claude Simon?

> All too intellectual for me. With a theory of literature to keep to and all imagination to be subordinated to it. Personally, I've never had ideas in that regard, never had anything to teach . . .
>
> Nathalie Sarraute is one of my very dearest friends. Of course, I've always thought her essays—on Dostoyevsky, for example[3]—were better than her novels, which are always too cerebral. A few years ago she also started to

write in an autobiographical style. But who among us has read *Childhood*? Word has it she sold very few copies.[4] Robbe-Grillet's got to the third volume of his family saga.[5] But tell me, do they still talk about his books in Italy? Agreed, he's a very brilliant man, an enthusiast . . . I remember one time when, a little bit confusedly, as was his way and no doubt with no ill intentions, he accused me of being repetitive.[6] As though dwelling on certain subjects, from one book to another, necessarily meant lacking imagination. Every new text I produce replaces the old one, amplifies it, modifies it.

There was talk in the 1950s, at the time of novels like The Sea Wall *or* Moderato Cantabile, *of some stylistic and thematic affinities between yourself and the* École du Regard.

That's not a topic I like to discuss. I simply say that my masters are and always will be other writers: Hemingway's dialogue, Mme de La Fayette's and Benjamin Constant's analyses of love, and then Faulkner, Musil, Rousseau . . .

What do you think of some contemporary French writers, such as Philippe Sollers, Michel Tournier, Michel Leiris, Michel Butor?

Who reads them? My suspicion is that they're boring. When it comes to people like Butor, after *La Modification* I don't think he had much to say. Sollers is too limited:[7] someone like him, who does all he can to attract the general public and get himself talked about by scandalizing the bourgeoisie with subjects that don't actually shock anyone any more, can't have much confidence in himself.

And then, I believe, those people can't stand me any more. They're envious, like most of the critics, who are up in arms every time I write in the newspapers or appear on TV, ready to attack me as they did last year when [Jean-Luc] Godard and I talked about books and cinema on TV.[8]

At any rate, none of them will ever write a book like *The Ravishing of Lol V. Stein*.

Do you know the 'New Philosophers'?

I don't dislike them, quite the reverse. But they merely seem to be rather provincial young men, afflicted with Parisianism and Left-wing snobbery. There doesn't seem to be much else to say about them, particularly for someone like me who lived through times of a completely different order of cultural depth.

Before Marguerite Yourcenar died, they said that the two of you were the foremost women writers in French.

Yourcenar was a member of the Académie française, I wasn't. What else is there to say? *Memoirs of Hadrian* is a great book. The rest, apart from *How Many Years?*, are, to my mind, unreadable. I gave up on them halfway through.

I was sometimes mistaken for her in the street. You're the Belgian novelist, aren't you? Yes, yes, I'd reply and then I'd slip away.

What do you think of committed literature, such as the work of Albert Camus?

As I've said, my contemporaries bore me. In most cases. I worked out that all his books had been constructed the same way, using the same trick, with the same moralizing objective. I find the very idea that literature can be conceived as a way of supporting an argument boring beyond words.

Let's come to your relationship with [Jean-Paul] Sartre.

I think Sartre is the reason for the regrettable cultural and political backwardness of France. He saw himself as Marx's heir, as the only true interpreter of his thought—that's where the ambiguities of existentialism come from. If you think of someone like [Joseph] Conrad, you can't even talk about Sartre as a real writer. Now he's just an isolated figure, huddled away in a kind of enforced exile. Before the war, the intellectual had to join the Party, as I did myself, but instead of the activism he should have been engaged in, Sartre took issue with the alleged 'sins of the intellectual'—sins that were primarily his.[9]

Among your regular visitors in the 1950s, there was also Georges Bataille.

We were very good friends, but nothing will ever shake my conviction—or at least my suspicion—that Bataille had something very Catholic in him. There's a sort of ambiguity runs that through all his work, as though he'd been tormented by a very old sense of guilt that both repelled and fascinated him at the same time. His erotic writings confirm this—and yet they deal with an external transgression. They have more to do with a sterile *jouissance* on paper, than a living *jouissance* felt in one's body.

As for his use of language, Bataille's greatness lies in his way of 'not writing' while still writing.

The absence of style in *The Blue of Noon* has to do with wanting at all costs to blank out all literary memory within oneself. In a sense, restoring a primal value to words, shorn of all their other implications. Similarly, the characters in the book, freed from the dross of bourgeois individualism, are moving towards annihilation, towards the dissolution of the 'self'.

You've spent a lot of time with Italian writers and intellectuals like Elio Vittorini, Italo Calvino, Cesare Pavese and Giulio Einaudi.[10] *You know Italy well from having spent a large part of your holidays there in the 1950s and 60s. What do you think of contemporary Italian literature?*

I stopped reading it in the mid 60s. Obviously, there was Vitaliano Brancati, Italo Svevo and Carlo Emilio Gadda. To be truly great, Vittorini should have left Italy, should have become less provincial, do you see?

Your liking for Elsa Morante is well known.

That's right. *La Storia*, that story of a woman walking alone in the bombed-out streets of Rome with her dog and her child—that's an image I can't get out of my head. I think I loved Morante for that and just when I'd have liked to have met her to talk about her novel, she died before I could tell her.[11]

• • • THE CRITICS • • •

. . .

When were your books first talked about?

In 1958, with *Moderato Cantabile*. The critics were divided about the book and that's how it's always been ever since. Some trotted out the *nouveau roman* label, speaking of 'a story that isn't a story'.

And then there were years of silence and lack of interest in your work on the part of most critics and a large part of the public. Then, suddenly, in 1984 came the Duras phenomenon: The Lover sold a million and a half copies in France alone. It was translated into twenty-six languages. How do you explain this sudden turnabout?

Every time a book comes out, the critics make the author feel in the wrong. They make her feel she needs to justify her work—and even her existence. With me, here in France, that's always how it's been. We've had enough of that now. It isn't me or my writing that have changed, but the public. Nowadays people also read hard, difficult things. And if they don't understand them, if they only grasp what's *said*, what's clear in a text, they carry on all the same, they get beyond the obscure passages. You advance by jumps in modern literature, from light to obscurity. And it's the same with scientific progress. Even if we don't know where and how far to advance, we advance all the same.

At the age of seventy, The Lover *won you the most prestigious of literary awards, the Prix Goncourt.*

Awarding it to me—simply because there was no valid reason not to—is a political matter: it was the beginning of a new conception of the meaning of that prize, which was traditionally given to young writers to encourage the production of literature.

Even among those around the Goncourt, you feel the influence of this 'Mitterand Era', in which everyone wants to conform . . .

For almost ten years I lived off my German royalties. Then I moved on to the royalties from Britain. I was a clandestine figure in France. I was subject to a kind of blackout.

And what brings me closer to the other women who write, who really write—from Colette onwards—is this way of feeling like an *enfant terrible* of literature. The critics have always been harsh on everything coming from certain female domains: the themes of love, confession and auto-biography. For years, women's transgression was expressed in—and confined to—poetry. I wanted to transfer it to the novel and a lot of what I've done is, I think, revolutionary.

What do you think of literary prizes?

My ideal would be a prize that put an end to that all-powerful criticism which is, in France, subject to the rules of power, where it's about the institution even more than the literary value of a work. The prize itself becomes the aim of writing. You would have to be able to judge the prize-jury first, to ensure that innovative intentions were to the fore. That's why I refused to take part in the panel judging the Prix Médicis when they asked me to. And the prize they awarded to Claude Ollier wasn't enough to make me change my mind.

Has the blackout you spoke about just now conditioned how you write?

No. My literature had an imperative force of its own. Doubts, if I had any, were about the writing itself, not the subject matter of my books. It was enough for me that, without even having to force them on the reader, certain things happened in people's heads.

There are readers today who, when they think of you, think first and foremost of your earliest books.

A host of old readers take me to task for 'not being so simple as in the past.' I can't say they're wrong. *The Lover*, *The Malady of Death* and *Emily L.* are difficult books, where the text advances by ellipses, silences and innuendo. An almost amatory collusion between text and reader is needed that's able to go beyond mere understanding of the sentences in themselves.

Would you like to lay out a set of instructions for how to 'read Duras'?

A non-continuous reading which, by contrast with the reader's normal habits, proceeds by jumps, jumps in temperature. Unlike the classic novel of the Balzac type, which is linear, these are open, unfinished books that are aimed, ultimately, at an evolving world, a world constantly on the move.

Don't you think there can be ways of educating people, of orienting them towards certain precise models for reading?

The best thing is to let certain processes happen on their own.

Do you think there have been misunderstandings between you and your readers in recent years?

If that's the case, they're over morality, not literature. Take the case of *The Lover*. What I find extraordinary in the life of the young white girl has been seen as aberrant by a lot of mothers.

Judging from the precautionary remarks you've made in the opening pages of your most recent books or on their back covers—defences, as it were, of the texts themselves—it would seem at all events that you need a lot of attention from the public.

I'm obsessed by the idea that my books aren't liked. Once I know that's not the case I calm down and stop thinking about it, but I don't find it easy to forget the scathing reviews. In 1964, *The Ravishing* was criticized and many long years afterwards, when the same newspaper—I won't say its name—asked me to write for it, I couldn't get that out of my mind.

In Destroy, She Said *and even in* Nathalie Granger, *some characters imply that books might be torn up and thrown away, even making downright calls for that to be done—emphatic calls at that.*

I thought it was necessary to destroy knowledge, to free oneself from it so as to be able to recreate it. Now I believe that one should only tear up books after having read an enormous amount. And then accumulate them again straight afterwards.

And how do you read?

I read at night, until three or four in the morning. The darkness around you adds greatly to the absolute passion that develops between you and the book. Don't you find that? In a way, daylight dissipates the intensity.

What do you read?

I've come back to *The Princesse de Clèves*, a book that's always read too quickly. It's a very fine book that I'd like to have written myself. Its extraordinary modernity lies precisely in that paroxystic play of gazes that cross without ever meeting, those words they exchange without ever really pronouncing them, those interminable silences in which, in reality, the unspeakable depth of the truth is hidden, as in any love affair. Then there are, of course, the books that always go with me: *Moby Dick, The Man Without Qualities,* the Bible. I'm currently rereading Jean-Jacques

Rousseau's *Confessions* and Jules Renard's *Journal*—the notebooks of the great writers, summations of a whole life and an entire period, make for an extraordinary read, disordered as they are and untrammelled by narrative structures.

As for the essay, once the great heritage of French literary endeavour, I find that, even in the case of some great practitioners like Jacques Le Goff and Georges Duby they keep trotting out concepts like 'ignorance and doubt' which, in themselves, have nothing creative about them any more. They're no longer going anywhere.

• • • A GALLERY OF CHARACTERS • • •

...

The deepest way to get inside someone, as Marguerite Yourcenar sees it, is 'to work to hear ... to create a silence within yourself in order to hear what ... [a character] would say in a particular situation. And you must take care never to put in your own voice, or at least see to it that what you do put in of yourself is at the level of the unconscious: you nourish your characters with your being as you might feed them your flesh, which is not at all same thing as feeding them your own petty personality with all the idiosyncrasies that make us who we are.'[1] What technique do you use in the construction of these recurrent characters in the world of your novels and films?

The image forms slowly, as though there were faded photographs to reconstitute from the surviving details by looking and imagining. It's never the whole shape or the expression on a character's face I manage to see. There are at best a few shreds of detail or just a simple characteristic gesture, as in Cubist painting.

Your characters lie beyond typologies or objective descriptions. They're beings disconnected from any reality, contingency or definition. Enigmatic, hovering between madness and normality, screaming and silence, they emerge suddenly on the scene without any of that inevitability and necessity that normally underpin the classic mechanisms of fiction. A form of ceremonial, something ritualistic pervades their actions and the unremitting flow of their speech. But there is no defined psychological framework for the individual character.

The hero of the traditional, Balzacian novel possesses an identity that's all his own, a smooth, unassailable identity pre-established by the narrator. But human beings are just bundles of disconnected drives and literature should render them as such.

Your work is based more on the dismembering of the personality of your protagonists than on their progressive construction.

I lay hold of them at this unfinished stage of their construction and deconstruction, because what interest me is the study of the cracks, of the unfillable blanks that emerge between word and action, of the residues to be found between what's said and what remains unsaid.

More than any other form of expression, it is dialogue that gives the characters their shape. What precedes the essence of their deep natures, the flow of consciousnesses, is the image of an existence evaluated only through spoken words and contingent action. The inner urgency that drives the characters isn't revealed or even analysed.

With the result that the reader will never be able to identify with them, contrary to what is usually done, by yielding to a surface psychologism. But the words my characters speak—like the words all characters speak, perhaps—

conceals their essence more than it reveals it. All they try to say and think is merely the attempt to muffle their own true voices.

If the male characters most often embody aspects of a weak, uncertain personality—I'm thinking of the Vice Consul of Lahore, Monsieur Jo, Jacques Hold, Chauvin, Michael Richardson[2] and the travelling salesman in The Square—*it's the female roles you endow with strength and with the radical need to experience the full gamut of feelings.*

Yes, women are the true guardians of a total openness to the external world, to life and to the overwhelming force of passion. I think that's why women are more directed towards the future and forms of life that renew themselves, like the silent heroines of *The Malady of Death*, *Blue Eyes*, *Black Hair* and *Emily L.* Men are more fossilized in pasts they can't shake off, they are prisoners of a desire they'd like to indulge but, hopelessly, cannot. By contrast, all the heroines of my films and books are like sisters of Andromache, Phaedra or Berenice—they are martyrs to a love that overwhelms them, to the point where it touches on the sacred.

The host of men and women that populate your books seem to derive from an archetype that is part of all of them to some extent. Anne-Marie Stretter and Lol V. Stein might be said to represent the genesis of the feminine archetype and the Vice Consul of Lahore the genesis of the male characters.

Lol is emblematic of a woman brought down by eternal desire, crushed definitively by the weight of her experience and memory. Though Lol goes on living after the ball at S. Thala, she leads an existence that enfolds her only as something alien, something bound up solely with her body or with animal instinct. For her, repressing her pain means acquiring a kind of new virginity, to the point where she has to remember everything each day as though for the first time. As for Anne-Marie Stretter, I truly do believe that I began writing for her—as though what I wrote had been simply the incessant rewriting of the fascination I felt, one day, for the almost deathly languor of that woman. I remember the first time I saw her arrive; she was the wife of the French ambassador at Saigon. She got out of a big black car. In a low-cut dress that revealed her slim, white body and with her French hairstyle, she stepped lightly and slowly along the road. I kept up a watch on her after that. I saw her leaving her home as soon as the sun went down and the heat abated, her beauty beyond my imagining.

The news that, for the love of her, a man—her young lover—had killed himself in Luang Prabang, Laos, disturbed me greatly. As mother and adultress, the woman became my personal secret from that point on—she was the feminine, maternal archetype that my mother never was, being too crazy to be that.

In the Vice Consul, by contrast—and, indeed, in many of the other men in my books, from the Chinese lover to the man in *The Malady of Death*—there was such great pain and weakness, an inability to live, based precisely on the total rejection of self and society. That, at least, is how my adolescent eye saw it. The impossible love affair between Anne-Marie Stretter and him represents, from that moment on, the story of absolute love and of the totality of colonial India.

The Durassian universe is static and stifling. It's a confined space that not even the reader feels he can escape. One only has to think of the area bounded by the mountains and the sea in The Little Horses of Tarquinia, *the forest in* The Sea Wall *and* Destroy, She Said *and the bare rooms in many of your novels where the lovers express their desire.*

The humanity I speak of finds our world hard to bear. They are only able to get beyond the neurosis paralysing them by an extreme act, like Alissa in *Destroy*, or, like everyone else, by renunciation. The places where that happens reflect that anxiety they feel.

Nothing of what happens outside, far from the chasms of the characters' minds, from their silences and the random character of their remarks, seems to concern them.

As regards the outside world, except for some exotic aspects (the Indochina of your first novels) or a vague historical context (the colonial question which shows through in The Sea Wall, *the war that forms the backdrop to* Hiroshima mon amour *or the student protest in* Destroy, She Said), *you allude to it only vaguely.*

The outside world interests me only by its effect on the minds of my characters. Everything happens, irremediably, in the stifling microcosm of the 'self'.

• • • CINEMA • • •

* * *

Do you often go to the cinema?

> Not much any more. In the films I watch on video with
> Yann, nothing seems very striking, there's nothing life-
> changing. You see quite a few good film-makers, excellent
> technicians but they're incapable of inventing a new lan-
> guage, even at the risk, perhaps, of getting some things
> wrong.

If, as you say, 'people go to the cinema to feel less alone and to be told sto-
ries', what do you think of dependence on television?

> Television is required watching. You have to watch it every
> day, as I do closely, even though I know it's hollow chatter,
> flattened reality. To watch the news broadcasts, the variety
> shows and the sporting contests is to stay in among other
> people and overcome the distance from parts of our age
> which one would otherwise never know about. Clearly,
> there are passive viewers. Who watch to spare themselves
> the effort of reading or speaking.

When you arrange to meet friends in Paris, it's invariably for at least a week ahead—all you have to communicate with at night is the telephone.

The television is often on in your flat. You and Yann follow the sport, don't you?

In May 1985, when there was the bloody riot at the Heysel Stadium in Belgium,[1] I was watching TV and saw the whole thing live. I thought I was going mad watching that convulsive whirl of images. I was there, but to no avail. I started shouting.

Two years ago in France there was quite a lot of talk about a meeting you had with Michel Platini,[2] an interview which you published in the sports pages of Libération *(of 14-15 December 1987).[3]*

I'd followed Platini for years, in all his matches. I liked and admired him. I find that football has that power—it triggers in the player, and perhaps in the spectator, that strong sense of humanity, that slightly childish truth that even now I find affecting in men.

And now let's turn to your films. La Musica *in 1966 was your first.[4] What do you remember of your beginnings as a film-maker?*

From the start I wanted to define a *Duras-style cinema*—a language that would be my own, without any fear. And that couldn't be seen as derivative of any of my masters.

Did you believe in the possibility of a new cinema?

Of a different cinema, certainly. In the sense of it being a medium that remained, in part, to be explored.

What were your first concerns when it came to trying to translate your written evocations into film?

> I wanted to render silence. A rich, living silence. Like something you might have been able to hear.

Do you still endorse what you wrote some years ago about your film-making? 'I make films to occupy my time. If I had the strength to do nothing, I wouldn't do anything at all. It's because I don't have the strength to do nothing that I make films. There isn't any other reason. There is nothing truer I can say about my enterprise.'[5]

> Yes.

Almost twenty films and as many novels.[6] What are the differences between your activity as a writer and as a film-maker?

> By its 'external' nature—being a collective work, a way of being *in* life, *with* other people—film doesn't have that urgency, that obsession that there is in writing. It might be said that the film distances the author from her work, whereas writing, woven out of silences and absences, throws her irremediably inside it. No one is as alone as a writer.

> I've often made films to escape that frightening, interminable, unhappy work. And yet I've always wanted more than anything else to write.

Could your writing be read as an 'infinite text', that is to say, a text that burgeons out from itself and from your memory, that spills over beyond its own context—in other words, from the page to film?

It was as though the word I wrote already contained its image within itself. To film it was to pursue the discourse and amplify it. It was to continue writing—on the image. It wasn't a question of betraying the sacred halo of the text but heightening it, discovering the whole of its physical presence.

How can your cinematographic work be characterized?

The reality reproduced by classical cinema has never been of any interest to me. Everything is *said* too much, shown too much—an excess of meaning in which, paradoxically, the context becomes impoverished.

In my films I don't gloss over or suppress those things that aren't functional or organic to the expressive unity of the fiction—they are made up of a material that's lacerated, superimposed, offset in time; there are gaps and breaks—that whole imaginary that's meant to render the heterogeneity and irreducibility of life.

There's a passage in *The Man Without Qualities* that sums up the sense of what I'm saying here:

> [I]t struck him that when one is overburdened and dreams of simplifying one's life, the basic law of this life, the law one longs for, is nothing other than that of narrative order, the simple order that enables one to say: 'First this happened and then that happened . . .' It is the simple sequence of events in which the overwhelmingly manifold nature of things is

represented, in a unidimensional order, as a mathematician would say, stringing all that has occurred in space and time on a single thread, which calms us; that celebrated 'thread of the story,' which is, it seems, the thread of life itself. Lucky the man who can say 'when,' 'before,' and 'after'! . . . It now came to Ulrich that he had lost this elementary, narrative mode of thought to which private life still clings, even though everything in public life has already ceased to be narrative and no longer follows a thread, but instead spreads out as an infinitely interwoven surface.[7]

Your films have been criticized for being excessively literary. It's a cinema, they say, that concedes too much to the slow indeterminacy of each sequence.

The inner time I want to recreate on film has nothing to do with 'narrative' time as it's normally understood in a film.

Because of the extensive use you make of sequence and panoramic shots, of fading to black and the stillness of each separate scene—all determined by a certain immobility of the camera—your films have been described as 'non-cinema' or 'anti-cinema'.

The static nature of the scene is merely apparent. Like the whirl of currents beneath the still surface of the sea or the murmur of voices hidden behind silences. They say that cinema is movement. Fine, but some words, some looks, some silences move as much as two men fighting or walking.

What is 'true' cinema for you?

I believe its essence lies in archaic, spare, elementary forms. This is why I've tried to bring cinema back to a zero degree of its expression, to an almost primitive state. To suggest, not to define. Without impoverishing cinema, by making it akin to certain artistic outcomes that were already achieved by silent movies in the time of the Lumière brothers or Marcel L'Herbier.

At the dawn of cinema, black-and-white film, for example, had an intensity—take [Carl Th.] Dreyer or [F. W.] Murnau—that colour will never have.

I'd like to get back to these blanks, these dramatic contrasts. As for colour, I'd like to use it to characterize certain aspects of reality, not to embellish that reality in order to gain a greater hold over the viewer.

You've always made 'low-budget' films. If you'd had more funding, would you have changed register?

No, meagre resources—thirteen million old francs for *Le Camion*, seventeen million for *Son nom de Venise dans Calcutta désert*[8]—sit well with the nature of the reality I've described. A reality that's ragged and hollowed out. I believe the beauty of the films also had to do with the small budgets and the very small amount of time I had available (sometimes as little as a week) to make them.

As on the page, then, the operation was aimed at paring or stripping down the narrative material?

I confined myself to eliminating the superfluous, what are called the 'hinge events' which normally serve to connect the different sequences together in a film, giving the whole context that sense of 'naturalness', that illusion of reality. By contrast, it was always my aim to stimulate the spectators' minds by forcing them to make an effort to put together those things which had previously been offered up to them as something unified and, as it were, pre-digested.

For what type of spectator did you make your films?

For the fifteen thousand people who like my cinema. There's a precise category of infantile filmgoers I'll never reach, who regard cinema as a pastime, as escapism.[9]

You yourself have experienced the intolerance of many viewers during the projection of your films. Have you been affected by that lack of popularity?[10]

Destroy, She Said was the first film where I realized, twenty years ago, that I wasn't interested in consensus. The producers wanted to dissuade me from putting my neck on the line once again: 'Are you sure what you're doing?' they asked. A lot of friends, though liking me as a writer, couldn't bear my film-making. They asked me why I needed to do it.

I didn't even reply. People can't understand that you can do something while knowing it's not worth the trouble.

And if the press ignored me, students are still writing theses about my cinema.

On the back cover of two of your most recent books, The War: A Memoir *and* Blue Eyes, Black Hair, *you urge your readers to read the text as something absolutely true.*

By contrast, when your highly controversial film L'Homme atlantique *came out, you published an article in* Le Monde *aimed at deterring people from going to see it. Provocatively, you demand from them a total, unconditional participation—a sort of devotion to, or faith in, your work.*[11]

I did, in fact, want to dissuade people from seeing that film. It wasn't worth it. They were going to be bored to death. For almost its entire duration (thirty minutes out of forty-five), the screen stays black.

How did you use the camera?

As though it were my own gaze projected outwards—remaining faithful to the subtlest little movements of that gaze. Just as I reject the role of classic novelist, omniscient and omnipresent, so I reject this invasion of the camera which dominates, imprisons and objectifies the action from above. The camera must be flexible, privileging the multiplicity of events; it must take different, interchangeable roles, moving with the same imperceptible mobility as the eyes of the characters. The camera is there to follow them, not to replace them.

What role did the editing phase have for you?

It was fundamental. The dark room in which you cut up the film and where it's reassembled in solitude and silence, painfully slowly, resembles the process of writing itself. There's the same ceremonial. With cinema, as on the page, the key thing is to delete. One should film little—just what's necessary. Giving the viewer as little to see as possible, and as much as possible to understand and listen to.

Listen to?

I sometimes realized, as I was filming, that everything my actors were saying was less important than the timbre of their voices.

You put your own voice on the soundtrack as a voice-over.

Bruno Nuytten, who was in charge of cinematography on a great many of my films, argued that it was very attractive on account of its tonality in G.

In the short films you made in 1978-79—Césarée, Les Mains negatives, Aurélia Steiner (Melbourne) and Aurélia Steiner (Vancouver)—a text read by yourself provides a commentary on images shot outdoors, which, in many cases, don't correspond at all to what's being said.

Often in your films there's a discrepancy—if not, indeed, a dissociation—between image and text. A constant slippage between shots, backgrounds and perspectives. Instead of illustrating dialogues or monologues, the visual content of the film might be said to evoke other meanings. Words themselves have lost all function of explanation or commentary.

It's as though the voices don't know the content of the images. Hence the narrative will never be immediate, direct. It will be up to the viewer to reconstruct it.

The screenplay, enriched with these syntactic jumps—from the present to the conditional, to the simple past—which don't sit easily with classical narration, emphasizes just this distantiation.

Le Camion is perhaps the best example of what you're talking about here. The cinematographic event—the screenplay that you and Depardieu are content just to read—subsists and can be described simply as a support that 'shows' the words, free of any concession to the novelistic.

Initially the film was supposed to be interpreted by actors playing roles. If I remember rightly, I had Simone Signoret in mind. But I wasn't entirely convinced by the idea. One night, I decided to tell the film rather than making it, reading it as it would have been *if* I had made it.

In films like L'Homme atlantique *and* Le Camion, *you used a black screen as an interruption—and, at the same time, a dissolution—of the meaning of everything that had been narrated to that point.*

I didn't want any pleonasms between text and image, but simply stretches of *black*, exactly like those *blank* spaces I put into my written narration.

What advice would you give to a film-maker who was starting out?

To find their own path without following any model or reference that would merely serve to conceal their own fear. In Italy—at Rome, at Taormina—I've been on the judging panels for many prizes. It's important that people in the film world make themselves seen; at any rate, these are regenerative places to meet and find stimulation. I must admit, I've found a lot of first films boring. An individuality only emerges at around the age of twenty-seven or twenty-eight. A film-maker only acquires it with his second film. Anyone is capable of making a first film.

What do you think of contemporary French cinema?

It's not possible to speak of a 'new French cinema' in the same way as people have talked of a 'new German cinema'. There's a sort of prevailing neo-romanticism and there isn't the innovativeness there once was . . . I suspect the latest generation of directors have lost the taste for reading. They don't read anything but screenplays and they read those in a reductive, superficial way, with an eye to the film they want to get out of them. And then there are *auteurs* of the Jean-Pierre Melville type, which is a relatively fashionable genre at the moment—'very French', as they say in other countries. It's an—entirely calculated—cinema based on 'look', based entirely on appearances.

French cinema for me is still the wonderful jokes and comical expressions of a Jacques Tati—and then Robert Bresson and Jean-Luc Godard. Godard is one of the very greatest. We are friends, even if we argue a lot. We have a high regard for each other, but are, I think, very different. That's why I refused to take part in his *Every Man for Himself/Slow Motion* and I didn't allow him to make the film of *The War: A Memoir*, which he would have liked to do. I'd have preferred it to be done by John Huston. With Bresson, frankly more than with any other film-maker, I feel the same emotion, the same intensity of pain as though each time I saw a film by him, it was the first one I'd seen. As for Jean Renoir, despite his dealing with subjects close to my heart—love, India—I find him too sentimental.

What about Italian cinema?

In France, there's still the myth of a certain neo-realism, à la [Roberto] Rossellini. Agreed, he was a great director, but I've never shared all that enthusiasm. I prefer those films of his that no one ever mentions, such as *The Rise of Louis XIV*. Have you seen that?

It might be thought there's something in common between [Michelangelo] Antonioni's films and your own.

If we're thinking of the opening shots of *L'Avventura*, then yes, I agree.

Do you know [Pier Paolo] Pasolini's work?

I've always been irritated by that aura of mysticism and all the rhetoric surrounding him as an individual. As for *Salò*, I found it downright revolting. That's why I've never had any desire to read his books.[12]

Tell me some more about your favourite film-makers.

When I used to talk with the *Cahiers du cinéma* group, I'd compare the love I have for Dreyer's tragic sublime with the intolerance I feel for [Ingmar] Bergman-style cerebral aestheticism. Sham stuff aimed at Americans wanting to sate their insatiable hunger for 'culture'.

My favourites are, and always will be, Yasujiro Ozu, John Ford, Jean Renoir and Fritz Lang. And Chaplin—his genius lies in his ability to say so many things without speaking. His eye movements, facial expressions, gestures and silences. How different from the Woody Allen–style obsession with words so typical of New York. Talkies will never have the intensity of the silents.

I recently read a long interview you did with Elia Kazan.[13]

Speaking to him, I noticed how alike we were.[14] The same, rather primitive, taste for the essential, for rigour and the cleanness of the image.

With me, Kazan is perhaps the only film-maker—the fact he's a man makes this even more extraordinary—to have attempted to represent desire. Ineffable and inaccessible by nature.

You wrote a whole issue of the magazine Les Cahiers du cinéma, *an issue entitled 'Les yeux verts' or 'Green Eyes'.[15]*

That began with a series of interviews they did with me. Then they wanted some direct contributions. In the end, it was decided that I'd coordinate the whole issue that was entirely devoted to me.

I suppose it was quicker in the end?

It was Godard who suggested this. To begin with, the editors did only a small print run. They didn't think it would sell. Now they've brought it out as a paperback.[16] They've told me it's doing very well . . . They've told me that the money that was down to me from sales—and I'm sure this is true—was just about enough to pay off the journal's debts.

Do you think your films can be regarded as works of women's cinema?

If I'd made 'women's' films, I'd have betrayed both—women and film. Except where their particular irony is concerned, the particular view they alone have of things, women really have to give up on the female part of themselves.

They must simply be authors, full stop. Going beyond the alienation of their role, which has always strengthened their position, but also undermined them.

Do you believe in political cinema?

If it's used badly, as in propaganda films, it can become a dangerous instrument. It's easier to convey messages and disseminate them through film than through books—the image simplifies what reading renders inimical. My films are all political in nature, but they don't talk about politics, they don't advance arguments. At least, their political meaning has to be achieved by other means—not those of rhetoric or the mythification of the proletariat.

René Clément made The Sea Wall *(also known as* This Angry Age) *in 1957, Peter Brook made* Moderato Cantabile *in 1960, Jules Dassin made* 10:30 P.M. Summer *in 1966, and Tony Richardson made* The Sailor from Gibraltar *in 1967. Then in 1985 there was the film Peter Handke made from* The Malady of Death. *And there was also Henri Colpi's* Une aussi longue absence (The Long Absence), *on which you*

collaborated. Not forgetting Hiroshima mon amour *by Alain Resnais.*
What do you think of the films made from your novels or screenplays?

> I started making films because, apart from Resnais's, I
> didn't like the ones that were made from my books. I said
> to myself, let me see what I'm capable of—it would have
> been impossible to do worse.

So the film-makers can be said to have denatured or betrayed the texts?

> Mainly by banalizing them. By appropriating stories
> or reinventing them in novelistic form, without under-
> standing that these were starting points, evocations based
> more on the reduction or suspension of narration than on
> its saturation. They tried to fill the gaps in the written
> text. But that way the words lost all their intensity—the
> image in their films was there precisely to substitute for
> the words, to illustrate the story by compensating for this
> paring-down.

> Cinema's been afraid of words for nearly fifty years
> now.

Paradoxically, the film that gained you recognition among the general
public was made from a scenario you authored, but not by you.

> Are you talking about *Hiroshima*? It was Alain Resnais who
> phoned me one day. I didn't even know he was thinking
> about filming it.

> Anyway, I provided him with all the direction and
> ideas. He followed me, backed me up. Godard was one

of the first to notice that the film—as is clear from the outset—is, first and foremost, my film.[17]

Did you and Resnais do a lot of work together?

I wrote the scenario and he reworked it as a function of ideas that came to him as he was working. He'd been to Japan to find ideas that we subsequently worked from.[18]

The film was made in 1959. Was that the first time you had been so closely involved in cinema?

Yes. I didn't know anything—about contracts or about percentages that should have come to me as royalties. In the process of producing a film, the author—even if she's mentioned and lauded by the critics—actually counts for nothing. Or she's treated merely as the narrator of a story that the film stages. I did a lot of work and was very poorly paid. I got a cheque for a million and a half old francs.[19] I thought I'd be getting more later on, but I came to realize that that was it. Resnais told me a few years later that I'd been given less than half of what I was owed. I was flat broke and inexperienced. Of course, no one helped me.

Your other very well-known film is India Song. *You yourself have spoken of it as a thwarting of any possible reconstruction.*

Yes, it was only through the destruction of the story that was told—the story of Anne-Marie Stretter and the Vice Consul—that another could be created, a story the wrong way round, that was even stronger. The whole film works by this distanced doubling.

And, after India Song, *what led you to make another film,* Son nom de
Venise dans Calcutta désert, *which not only uses the same soundtrack
but evokes the same settings, the same atmospheres?*

> For some months I'd felt a sense of dissatisfaction—a
> feeling I hadn't finished what I wanted to say with *India
> Song*, that I had something else to say. Anyway, both are the
> perfect staging of what I'd imagined when I was writing
> them—the decay of the French embassy in India is already,
> in itself, the end of colonialism, the despair of the whites,
> the exhaustion of a love affair, the twilight and death that
> I felt as a child walking down those streets.

Your last film, The Children, *with Pierre Arditi, André Dussollier and
Axel Bogousslavsky, was made in 1984. Since then, you've said you don't
want to make any more films.*

> That's true, yes. I'm done with cinema. After all, making
> films was difficult all those years.

*The film is about an adult-child Ernesto, who suddenly refuses to go to
school because he doesn't, as he puts it, want to learn what he doesn't
know. He's strenuously opposed to the logic of compulsory education.*

> Ernesto's madness, in a world wholly subject to the
> logic of consensus, lies in this excessive, extreme, revolu-
> tionary freedom he'd like to have; in his rejection of all pre-
> established values, in his desire to destroy and sabotage
> knowledge—in his case, academic knowledge—so as to
> recover universal innocence within himself. It's no acci-
> dent that the film is built on a sort of desperate comedy.

As you made it, were you thinking of your son Jean?

Yes, of Outa[20] and of myself. Ernesto, like me, has learnt to say no.

What were your relations like with the actors? Judging by your relationship with Gérard Depardieu in Le Camion *and when you directed Lucia Bosè and Jeanne Moreau in* Nathalie Granger, *one would imagine they were very intense.*

Even passionate. A thing of understandings and clashes. We talked about everything and I was often forced, as a result of the actors' criticisms, to change the text to accommodate their suggestions, adapting the characters to the actors playing them as we went along.

It was important to me that there was nothing general about their attitudes—that they came from themselves, the emotions and fears driving them. They said I was hard, that I got angry.

I even got mad with Yann, when he was working on *Agatha* with Bulle Ogier. I wanted him to 'enter into' the film, not to act it. Depardieu and I got on together straight away. Before we began, I simply said, 'Give in to the sound of the words you're speaking, without worrying about the meaning of the sentences. The music of the words, the tone you adopt will be enough to overcome the static nature of the film.' *Le Camion*'s a difficult film, yet we never had a moment's boredom or anguish. Depardieu and the team were enthusiastic.

You yourself have admitted that you had special relationships with actresses, from Jeanne Moreau and Lucia Bosè through Delphine Seyrig, Bulle Ogier, Madeleine Renaud and Dominique Sanda, to Isabelle Adjani and Catherine Sellers.[21] *And, indeed, many of them have become your friends.*

Madeleine Renaud is still one of my dearest friends. We are even alike in our rather hasty, careless way of dressing. I like to listen to her, rather than talk theatre with her. I love her guilelessness, her 'naive' innocence ([Samuel] Beckett once said that was her genius), the fact of knowing that even now walking on stage is a terrible ordeal for Madeleine.

You wrote Savannah Bay *for her.*

I couldn't forget the way she'd played the role of my mother in *Whole Days in the Trees*. She asked me to talk about her and I showed her some photos. It was really moving. Madeleine threw off her Parisian manner and became a teacher of native children in Indochina.

Suddenly I could see my mother there, old and drained, on the big stage at the Odéon theatre.[22]

In your bedroom, there's a big photo of Delphine Seyrig who was chosen by you to play in India Song—*and not accidentally.*

It was Resnais who discovered her. He wanted her to be in *Last Year in Marienbad*. That was in 1961. Delphine had been a theatre actress for eight years at that point. She was reclusive, reserved and didn't give interviews. She wasn't among the fashionable set and yet she was one of France's greatest actresses. Without having seen her, I believe I'd have chosen Delphine, just from hearing her on the telephone, for her extraordinary vocal inflections.[23]

In Nathalie Granger, *on the other hand, the actresses are Jeanne Moreau and Lucia Bosè. Did you write the screenplay with them in mind?*

I liked the idea of working with two big stars, but going against the clichéd approach—showing their bodies from behind, or their hands, but not lingering over their legs, faces or breasts.

I wanted to make a film that respected women's rhythms without appealing to the usual, hackneyed femininity. I've got good memories of the understanding that formed, as women, between them and me.

As for Jeanne, since the time of *Moderato Cantabile* I've been aware of the extraordinary intelligence in her eyes, the seriousness with which she entered into her roles. While she was making the film with Peter Brook, she kept coming to my place to ask for information about the life of Anne Desbaresdes, which I had to make up on the spot to satisfy her.[24]

Jeanne is a lot like me—we've both of us felt the force of a love throughout our entire lives. Not necessarily a love already in existence, but something that wasn't there yet, that was going to come—or to end.

• • • THEATRE • • •

. . .

You've written quite a lot of stage plays and adaptations. What happens when your works are adapted for the stage?

> Whereas a book exists as such, in this case it's the stage that 'lends reality' to a text which wouldn't exist at all on its own. It's the actors' voices that bring it to life, overriding even the voice of the author. Ultimately, I'm silent as my stage plays are performed—an unseen 'vanishing point' in the wings. The actors, as we might say, speak in my stead.

What's the difference between a theatre production and a film set?

> The theatre will never be an industrial product. It's something alive, a risk that begins afresh every evening. The cinema knows nothing of these fears; a film is vivisected and corrected before being offered up to the viewer.
>
> There's nothing chancy or fortuitous about it.

But there are the limits of the stage, which everyone knows. Only film allows you to give total free rein to the imagination.

That's exactly where the theatre scores—its limited scope of vision.

And what changes does the text undergo when it's staged? In your work, it would seem there aren't those inevitable slippages that usually happen when we move from book to film or to the stage. Critics have often presented your work as having no internal boundaries, no break in continuity, whatever art form you adopt.

To work in the theatre, a literary text has to be constructed very strictly. This is something that very seldom occurs. First and foremost, the scale has to be changed—one could confine oneself to the dialogues, but they aren't sufficient. Hence a certain difficulty in rendering certain ineffable evocations that have to do with the magic of the written text—evocations that film is also able to render, though to a lesser degree, by way of technical effects.

Take a text like *The Malady of Death*, entirely built around the blank spaces, the pauses, the gaps, the sound of the sea, the light, the wind—the stage is too small . . .

Who is the playwright you feel closest to?

Strindberg analyses the ghastliness of man's inner dejection. Pinter brings out humanity's pathology. But the theatrical space never conveys what really happens between human beings, except perhaps in the plays of Chekhov.

A theatre of text and voice, interwoven with apparently banal and yet significant details. It's beneath the 'simple' structure of the dialogues and what speech hides or masks—beneath the allusive stammerings of conversation—that the greatness of Chekhov lies. These are texts which, like mine, are never saturated; texts in which the action is suspended, left unfinished. A sort of music of silence. Entirely left to the imagination.

Thinking of texts like The Square, La Musica, L'Amante anglaise, Suzanna Andler, Savannah Bay *and* Whole Days in the Trees, *what genre do your plays belong to?*

There's no theatre without tragedy. And tragedy is love, hysteria . . . even the simple separation of a provincial couple. What I'd really like to do would be to transpose the sacred power of liturgy into theatrical speech.

You yourself have defined your theatrical productions as a 'theatre of spoken words and voices'.

The main thing is not to call it a 'theatre of ideas'.

What does it mean to you to have worked for the theatre?

It's about having learnt to treat the theatre as something foreign to oneself, something done and made outside of oneself, without the involvement and intimacy that normally comes about with a book. It was the dialogue I put enormous effort into. I rewrote it every day, for three hours each morning. Then I'd get to the theatre in the afternoon with new ideas each time. *La Musica*, for example, is one of the texts that underwent the most change. Until the day when Miou-Miou and Sami Frey were exhausted and asked me to stop . . .

How does your relationship with the actors in the theatre differ from your relations with film actors?

What they brought to the text was indispensable—more so than anywhere else. That's to say, it helped me to modify the text, even if that meant starting again from scratch, before it was acted in front of an audience.

Ideas, as I remember, emerged like that—simply from seeing someone's body move in a particular way.

What, in your view, should be the relationship between the text and the voice interpreting it?

The actor shouldn't identify with it in a naturalistic way but keep a certain distance, playing on the distantiation between person and character.

Where did this passion for the theatre come from?

Definitely not from any shows that I saw. In a village in Cochinchina in the 1930s there was neither cinema nor theatre. One of the rare publications to be found in our home was *La Petite Illustration*.[1]

You began to write plays in the 1950s with Les Viaducs de la Seine-et-Oise. *What did you think of French theatre at the time in the immediate aftermath of the war?*

Some of the theorists like Antonin Artaud, despite having revolutionized the theatre, didn't interest me all that much. As for Sartre and Camus, my impression was that they were making thesis-plays, a form as outdated as the ideologies they were replete with. A defective, didactic theatre that lacked the true contribution of tragedy. The spectators were reduced to the role of passive—subordinated, I would say—recipients of everything that was laid out before them.

At each opening night of a new Camus play, Dionys Mascolo forced me to go with him.[2]

What do you think of theatre criticism?

That it's only meaningful for a beginner—certainly not for someone like me. I've no time at all for the theatrical rearguard, based, as it was forty years ago, on criteria of psychological verisimilitude or things of that sort.

It even upsets me that the critics come to see my plays, mistaking the ferocious clashing of memories and passion for mawkish sentimentalism.

• • • PASSION • • •

. . .

All your books are love stories in one way or another. Passion as last and necessary recourse for transcending that powerlessness and that immobilism which paralyse your characters. As axis of the whole Duras world.

> Love remains the only thing that really counts. It is stupid to think of it as confined to what happens between a man and a woman.

Yourcenar criticized French literature for the dominant, obsessive character of the love theme.[1]

> I don't agree. Even if it's the main subject of all the arts, nothing has ever been so difficult to express and describe as passion: it's the most commonplace and, at the same time, the most ambiguous thing.

There's a line in Hiroshima mon amour *which perhaps sums up what you regard as the deep, contradictory nature of all love: 'You destroy me. You're so good for me.'[2]*

> It was when, as a poor, wayward creature, I met the Chinese lover that I discovered the ambivalence nestling in every passion. Love as desire to possess the other to the point of wishing to devour him.[3]

Speaking of The Lover, *you've described the affair with the rich Chinese as one of the most important of your entire life.*

All the other ones followed on from that—all the declared, codified love affairs. In the attempt to name it, lifting it out of its original, sacred obscurity, language kills all passion, contains it, diminishes it. But when love isn't *spoken*, it has the force of the body, the blind, undiminished force of *jouissance*: there remains the miraculous vision of the lovers, haloed in shadow. In *The Lover*, I could tell this story only from afar, speaking about the Chinese town, the rivers, the sky, the plight of the whites who lived there. About love I said nothing.

A total love, which fascinates and frightens at the same time, is searing. In The Square, *the girl says: 'Things happen like that. Things that cannot be avoided, that no one can avoid,' to which the man replies: 'Nothing is so worth living as the things which make one so unhappy.'*[4] *Something like the* amour fou *of the Surrealists, a passion that carries lovers beyond the prosaic nature of the everyday. As a search for the absolute, that alone can combat death, evil and* tedium vitae. *'There is no love affair in the world that can take the place of love. Nothing can be done about it,' says Sara, the heroine of* The Little Horses of Tarquinia.[5]

And it can only find peace or resolution in absence or death: 'I wish you were dead,' says Chauvin to Anne Desbaresdes in Moderato Cantabile.[6] *A total love precisely because it is, ontologically, impossible. In your short texts,* L'homme assis dans le couloir, L'Homme atlantique, La Pute de la côte normande *and in* Blue Eyes, Black Hair, *this aspect swells to the point where it becomes the metaphor for passion itself.*

Love exists for only a few moments. Then it disperses—into the very impossibility, the real impossibility, of changing the course of a life.

The love theme refers on to another, the inability of the sexes to communicate with each other. Your characters love one another and struggle constantly, only to fail in the end.

It isn't sex—what people are in a sort of sensual discolouration—that interests me. It's what lies at the origin of eroticism—desire. What one can't—perhaps what one shouldn't—allay with sex. Desire is a latent activity, in which respect it resembles writing—you desire the way you write, always.[7]

And, in fact, when I'm moving towards writing, I feel myself more invaded by writing than when I'm actually doing it. Between desire and jouissance there's the same difference as between the primal chaos of the written—which is total and unreadable—and the final result of what, on the page, is simplified and clarified.

Chaos is in desire. Jouissance is just that tiny part of what we've managed to attain. The rest—the enormity of what we desire—stays there, lost for ever.

Don't you believe this image of desire belongs to typically feminine worlds?

Perhaps. Male sexuality revolves around very precise models of behaviour—excitation, orgasm. Then you start again. There's nothing that remains in suspense and unsaid. Obviously, not all women, restrained as they are by ancestral principles of sterilizing faithfulness, are capable of living out the totality of desire without being made to feel guilty.

You've often argued that, even at the age of fifteen, the traces of desire were already visible on your face.[8]

As a young girl, from my first adventures, with strangers, between beach huts and in trains, I knew what desire meant.[9] With the Chinese lover, I felt the whole force of that and, since then, my sexual encounters have always been numerous—and even violent.

How did you manage to combine your countless passions with what might be called a real obsession with your work?

Each time in my life I stopped living with a man, I rediscovered myself. I wrote my finest books alone—or with passing lovers. Books produced in solitude, I would call those.

What do you think of men?

That they live in a sort of state where life is opaque to them—to the point where they don't notice most of the things around them. Caught up in themselves. In what they're doing—sometimes to the point where they never know what's going on noiselessly in a woman's head. There's still, I believe, a phallic group of men that take themselves so seriously . . .

How would you describe your life with men?

I've always followed them—on journeys, everywhere. Sharing the happiness they derived from the leisure they forced on me, which I couldn't bear. Otherwise, they would have been mad with rage. The men I've had found it hard to endure my incessant comments on my difficulties with writing, my moaning when the critics slated me. They wanted me to take care of the housework, the cooking and, if I really had to write books, to do it on an occasional basis, in a hole-and-corner way.

In the end I was always elsewhere—writers are never where others would like them to be.

I've known men of all kinds. They would, of course, all have liked me to write a bestseller. But not before the year 2000.

What faults do you find in men?

That you have to love them a great deal to put up with their need to wade in and have their say, to interpret everything that's happening around them.

You've often stated that 'men are all homosexuals'.[10]

Incapable of living the potency of passion to the full, I would add. Only prepared to understand those who are like them. A man's true life companion—his real confidant— can only be another man. In the male world, woman is elsewhere, in a world which man chooses to be part of from time to time.

What do you think of homosexuality?

Love between members of one's own sex lacks that mythic, universal dimension that belongs only to opposite sexes: even more than their lovers, homosexuals love homosexuality.[11] That is why literature—you only have to think of Proust—has had to convert homosexual passion into heterosexual—Alfred into Albertine, to be clear.

As I've said before, this is why I can't regard Roland Barthes as a great writer: something always limited him, as though the most ancient experience of life had passed him by, the sexual knowledge of a woman.[12]

Are you familiar with female homosexuality?

Of course. The pleasure another woman gives is something very intimate, which will always bear the stamp of an absence of dizzying passion. The stunning event, the one that can overwhelm us, is an encounter with a man.

In texts like The Malady of Death *and, even more so, in* Blue Eyes, Black Hair, *you take on dramatically and, at the same time, with great clearsightedness the theme of male homosexuality. The two books tell the story of a love that will never be able to happen between a woman and a man who finds himself incapable of deriving pleasure from her body.*

That's a question I know well. Like death, homosexuality is the exclusive domain of God, an area in which neither man nor psychoanalysis nor reason can intervene. And, indeed, the impossibility of procreation makes homosexuality very much akin to death.

You've even stated that you've known and loved many homosexuals.

I thought they were like other people before I knew them. But, in reality, they're not. The homosexual is alone, doomed to forego the company, except sporadically, of the person who is like him. The woman who lives alongside him will be alone at his side. And yet it's precisely at that point, where it would seem impossible—a radical, physiological impossibility—that love can be experienced. As happened in our case.

You've been living with Yann Andréa for nine years.

He sought me out. For two years he wrote me some beautiful letters. That wasn't a surprise. After reading my books, a lot of people did that.

I wasn't feeling well the day I decided (who knows why?) to reply to him. Then he phoned and, without having ever seen this student from Caen, I told him to come over. We quickly began drinking together and that's how our *folie à deux* began. Once again, I discovered, with Yann, that the worst thing that can happen in life is not to love.

I was overwhelmed by his presence. His friends were critical of him for staying with a woman far older than himself, but Yann paid no attention to that.

I still ask myself how it's possible. Our passion has been tragic, like all passions. And it was born out of that non-coincidence, that non-fulfilment of our desire.

Yann Andréa is the author of a book entitled M. D.—*its syncopated style is very reminiscent of your recent literary production—in which he*

*recounts the horrors of the detox and hospitalization you decided to
undergo some years ago.*[13]

> I very much recognize myself in that book. Studies of my
> films and books are published, but never books about
> myself, just as I am.

In what particular respect do you see yourself in it?

> In that sense of exhaustion, dissatisfaction, emptiness.
> That self-destruction by the mere thought of no longer
> being capable of living without drinking.

When was the first time you stopped?

> I knew alcohol the way you know a person. I'd begun
> drinking casually in political meetings or at parties. Then,
> at forty, I really hit the bottle. I stopped first in 1964, then
> I started again ten years later. I've started and stopped
> three times so far. Until I went into the American Hospital
> at Neuilly where, after three weeks of hallucinations, delir-
> ium and howling, they managed to pull me through.
>
> Seven years have gone by since then and yet I know I
> could start again tomorrow.

Why, in your opinion, do people begin drinking?

> Alcohol transfigures the ghosts of loneliness. It replaces
> the 'other' who isn't there. It stops up the holes that have
> opened up in us at some point, long ago.

• • • A WOMAN • • •

. . .

You once defined your life as a 'film that's been dubbed . . . badly cut, badly acted, badly put together. In short, a mistake. A whodunnit without either murders or cops or victims; without a subject; pointless.'[1]

At times I feel porous, spongy, permeated indiscriminately by everything going through my head.

There's a woman, the heroine of Le Camion, with whom perhaps you identify, who says she has a 'head full of wind'.[2]

Like the writer, this woman is a thing of availability to the outside. Ready to receive sudden bursts of strong sensation, as I am when I'm walking along the beach or in the countryside.

How would you define yourself?

As joyful. I like a laugh. I laugh because I find myself funny sometimes, or at stupid things that other people don't even notice. Of course, I can then fall back suddenly into that anxiety from when I was eight years old—fear of things, people, the vastness of the forest. When you're young, unsure of yourself and your existence, you set out in life lacking confidence. It's only later that you learn to trust in yourself, as though 'yourself' were another person.

Often in life, I've had the sense of not existing—having no models, no reference points—always looking for a place, never finding myself where I'd have liked to be, always late, always unable to enjoy the things other people enjoy. Nowadays, I like the idea of that multiplicity—we're always forcing ourselves to reach a oneness that's our lot, whereas our strength lies in this very exceeding of oneness.

If, today, at seventy-five, you were to take stock of your life overall ...

Without my childhood and adolescence, the desperate history of my family, the war, the Occupation and the concentration camps, I don't think there'd be much to my life. Working in Mitterand's department when he was minister for war veterans, I became aware of Hitler's atrocious crimes, Auschwitz and the extermination of seven million Jews.[3] I was thirty years old and it was only at that point, it seems to me, that I woke from a long sleep.

Do you see yourself as being alone?

Like everyone, I feel that ultimate loneliness which we all, from fear, try to cover up to the very end. But a day without being alone would seem stifling to me.

They say you still like to be among women and young people.

I've always enjoyed female company. I've always found it stimulating. I can remember whole afternoons chatting with my women friends. We laughed a lot and drank together.

With young people, it's different. I like them, though I have the impression I don't have much to teach them. Not even a theory of the novel . . . I prefer them to some old friends that I've stopped seeing, now that I don't have the same 'look' I once had. I'd had my fill of hearing myself being told, 'Marguerite, shut up please.'

Talking to me about your mother, you said, though you'd forgotten many things you'd read, many analyses and arguments, you hadn't forgotten her extraordinary stories.

That's just it. I often have the impression of forgetting the most urgent things—those I know I ought to keep in mind for one reason or another—and remembering nonsense or insignificant detail. A voice, a dress material . . . I've forgotten the articles I've written, the things I've said, the daily life I led for years. As though that was a host of events that had passed through my head on some parallel path, without leaving any trace. It's involuntary memory, not our will, that decides for us.

How has the fact of being a woman affected your work?

I've lived pain more or less as a state inherent in being female. Like all women, I've been bored or wearied living with men who either wanted me by them to help them rest from their work or wanted to leave me at home. And it was there, at home, in the kitchen that I often wrote. I grew to like the empty space left by men when they went out. It was only then I could think—or not think at all, which amounts to the same thing.

What you say there is reminiscent of certain states of mind of Sara in The Little Horses of Tarquinia.

> Sara's never alone. There's always the child with her or Jacques, her husband or the maid, or the 'other', the man who can—and won't—be her lover. In spite of that, her loneliness is the implacable loneliness of someone who stays silent. And in those silences everything happens.

What do you think is specifically feminine about your work?

> I don't ask myself the question what it means to have a feminine sensibility when I'm working.

In A Room of One's Own, *Virginia Woolf says the normal, perfect condition of every human being is one where the male and female principles live in harmony.*[4]

> The great mind is androgynous.[5] To aim to feminize art in certain ways is a great mistake on the part of women. By creating that specificity for themselves, they limit the very scope of their remarks.

What do you think of feminism?

> I'm wary of all these rather obtuse forms of activism that don't always lead to true female emancipation. There are counter-ideologies that are more codified than the ideology itself. Of course, a conscious, informed woman is already in herself political—provided that she doesn't confine herself to a ghetto by making her body the prime site of martyrdom.

Are we to understand, then, that silence, the practice and understanding of silence, are the very measure of feminine being?

> Instead of eliminating silence or fearing its ambiguity, women express and embrace the wholeness of silence in the words they speak. Where men are concerned, they feel *the imperative need to speak*, as though they couldn't bear the force of silence at all.

This different use of the spoken language between the sexes would seem to bring us back once again to the comparison you often allude to between women and witches.

> In *La Sorcière*, Michelet states that it was women's solitude that lay at the origins of their use of language.[6] Left to their own devices by men who'd gone off to the Crusades, the contention is that, once alone, they began to speak a primal ancestral, language with nature. Consequently, it's argued, to prevent the spread of non-codified speech, they were punished. Women—and children—have always been closest to transgression and madness.

In an essay he wrote on you, Dionys Mascolo has spoken of 'an extreme imprudence of which only a woman is capable, a penchant for risk-taking different from the kind that heroes of the "spiritual" life have accustomed us to, and the ability to question all certainties, our acquired sense of security, in a high-stake game which seems guided only by an inconceivable (unable to be conceptualized) confidence in the unknown as such.'[7]

> I'd add the ability to face up to the experience of pain without being destroyed by it. A certain weakness on men's part

renders them unprepared to such a degree that they shy away from the very substance of suffering by mythifying it, by expelling it from themselves with anger and physical violence.

The courage to get to the unvarnished truth doesn't prevent your female characters from also resorting to lying. They dissimulate almost as a matter of course. I'm thinking of Suzanna Andler, Sara, Anne Desbaresdes, Lol, Anne-Marie Stretter . . .

They are victims of passions within them—as in the case when, because of the Chinese lover, I began to lie to my mother. They are, above all, torn by a personality split that they don't understand.

How does a woman who, like you, writes, look back on the way she experienced motherhood?

A man will never be able to know what it means to put one's body at another's mercy to the point where one's energies are exhausted. With the awareness of the violence every act of giving birth has within it, by the very fact of knowing already what pain the person we are bringing into the world will go through.

What's your relationship with Jean Mascolo, the son you had on 30 June 1947 with Dionys Mascolo?

We're friends, Outa and I. He's one of the very few people who really know me. He knows my neuroses and my many hysterias.[8] And then he's an excellent travelling companion. We've never seen very much of each other when we've been in Paris, though we've sometimes met up in the evenings, but we've often travelled together in Europe. He was my escort, he protected my isolation. We complement each other—what with my obsession with work and his relaxed attitude to free time.

Jean Mascolo has often played a part, though indirectly, as cameraman or photographer, in the making of your recent films, such as The Children, *a story inspired—and this is no accident—by him.*

Up to now, he's been a jack of all trades, without ever finding anything that entirely absorbs him. Neither his father nor I have ever pushed him to find something. The money I have now belongs to him. I share it with him, like the times when I'm given something special to eat.

At the time of May '68, your son was involved in politics.

He was a real hippy. Gentle, indifferent, distant.

A bit like the indefatigable Alissa of Destroy, She Said.

If I hadn't learnt certain things from Outa, perhaps I'd never even have written that book.

How did you react to your son's commitment?

He went round to his father's to tell him that there was nothing he wanted to do or could do. Then he went away. For years, we'd see him coming back from Africa and going off there again, each time thinner, more emaciated. Yet we were happier knowing he was broke and workless than an anonymous prisoner of some office, waiting, like millions of people, for the alarm clock to ring in the early morning and send him off to the daily grind.

• • • PLACES • • •

· · ·

You produced a fine book of photos called Les lieux de Marguerite Duras [Marguerite Duras' Places] *devoted to your favourite locations—a sort of album of the mythic places of your personal geography.*[1]

> There are places in my memory which, more than others, trigger very strong passions in me: places I know even now that I couldn't pass through unscathed. The body recognizes them instinctively. The house at Vinh Long near the lake is, and always will be, linked to the discovery of pleasure, a discovery I'd never have been able to share with my mother.[2] It would have killed her.

In almost all your books, the presence of the sea is always perceptible, even if not always directly. It even makes an appearance as the subject of a slim diary-style narrative entitled L'Été 80 [Summer '80].[3]

> The sea is one of the images, one of the nightmares that recurs most frequently in my head.[4] Few people, I think, know it as I do, having spent hours observing it. The sea fascinates and terrifies me. I've been horrified since childhood by the idea of being swept away by water. But the real sea is the North Sea. And only Melville in *Moby Dick* has put its terrible threatening power into words.

Many of your characters, from Lol V. Stein onwards, live in seaside resorts or, at any rate, speak often of the sea.

The sea's an unlimited force that engulfs the 'self' and the gaze, each first losing themselves before they recover their own identity. At the end of the world, all that will be left to cover the earth's crust will be a single immense sea. All the feeble traces of humanity will have disappeared.

You spend a large part of the year in your flat in Trouville, alternating brief stays in Paris with spells at Neauphle-le-Château.

The Trouville flat's in an enormous, empty old hotel with large windows and a floor that's a chequerboard of black and white slabs. I associate a certain clear, cold light with the place, a light I find only there. And also the wind, the first moons of autumn and even the smell of the petrol refineries of Le Havre.

As for the house at Neauphle, I fell in love with it from the first. After so many wanderings, I was joyous, when I bought it, at the thought of having a house of my own for the first time. Living in it subsequently, as in a theatre that would in itself have demanded that stories be written for it, I thought of *Lol V. Stein* and *Nathalie Granger*.[5]

Resnais came to pick me up from there one day and opted to use it for Emmanuelle's flashbacks at Nevers in *Hiroshima mon amour*. Together we realized it is places that contain the image of future films. But there's no point determinedly seeking them out. You have, rather, to start from nothing and let the places speak to you, without any pre-existing idea.

And your current flat in the rue Saint-Benoît in Paris?

It's only changed once in forty years. Now I suppose it'll stay as it is.

The house is a receptacle you enter to be reassured and, at the same time, to be influenced, fundamentally and dangerously, by its occupants. It belongs to woman—man is happy just to use space—as a sort of extension of her womb. That's why it mustn't be cluttered with fetishes which, separating it from the outside world, render it unliveable. For me, the home has always been an open place, and the outside air has to be let into it. My whole life, though I was living alone, I never closed the door until late in the evening.

For years, your flat was a meeting point for a tight circle of friends.

Ah yes. Georges Bataille, Maurice Blanchot, Gilles Martinet, Edgar Morin and Elio Vittorini came here. They were friends, but when I wrote I wasn't thinking about them or what we discussed in the evenings.

I've always separated the two spheres: for them, I may perhaps have merely been a chatty, hospitable friend, inclined to let them sleep on the sofa and make them meals at any hour.

Your flat still gets a lot of visitors today.

People who call or come straight up and ring the doorbell. They say they want to see me. Personally, it never interested me to get to know the artists I liked. What they did was enough for me. So if I'd been asked, 'Do you want to meet Picasso?', I'd have said no.

A large proportion of artists haven't the slightest notion of the greatness or importance of their work. The sublime ignorance, as we might say, of Bach or Velasquez . . .

Do you like Paris?

It's become almost impossible for me to live there. The traffic horrifies me—I've stopped driving—and the city seems like a gigantic lethal, commercial labyrinth that's squandering its beauty day by day to conform to the norms of a supposed 'new architecture'.

Even the working-class areas are changing, such as Pigalle and the Marais. As are the suburbs, which used, at least, to teem with life. They've been transformed into enormous blocks of concrete where the isolation's even more atrocious, if that's possible.

The Paris I like is the deserted Paris of summer Sundays or the night, but that hardly exists any more.

Do the places you find yourself in at a particular time influence your work?

Yes. I'm finding it harder and harder to work in Paris. And not only because, opposite my windows—just over from my desk—they've knocked down a nineteenth-century printworks and put up a four-star hotel, a white hotel in the Broadway style.

The fact is that if I stayed in Paris, I'd probably be overwhelmed by the chaos and withdraw into my lair. Whereas what you need when you're writing is to smell the air, hear the sounds and be aware of everything that's alive—the outside world.

• NOTES •

• • INTRODUCTION

1   A former photographer of German origin, Inge was the widow of
    Giangiacomo Feltrinelli and one of Duras' publishers in Italy. (All
    footnotes to this volume are the work of the French translator, unless
    otherwise stated.—Trans.)

• • FRENCH TRANSLATOR'S NOTE

1   Michel Tournier, *Célébrations* (Paris: Gallimard, Collection folio, 2000),
    p. 305.

2   For a list of Duras' main interviews, see p. 180.

• • • A CHILDHOOD

1   Duras left Vietnam in 1932 and never returned.

• • • THE PARIS YEARS

1   Margeurite Duras, *Le Camion, suivi d'Entretien avec Michelle Porte* (Paris:
    Minuit, 1977), p. 115.

2   In an article in the *Nouvel Observateur* dated 12 January 1970, Sollers
    stood out against an overly political interpretation of May '68 and
    offered not a 'literary' but a psychoanalytic interpretation of the film
    (though not of the novel) around the theme of castration and (male
    and female) homosexuality:

    A woman is undergoing a sort of wild analysis from the
    three others and it might be said that she'll be sympto-
    matically 'cured' at the end of the film—there's a very fine
    token of this in her vomiting—but it is a cure that resolves
    nothing since it runs up against a social impossibility
    represented by the arrival of the 'husband'. And it is at that
    moment, I think, that the very impossibility of the *outside*

of the closed analytical space arises or, in other words, the dream of a sort of impossible community within that closed space. I find this interesting ideologically, because it is a problem that relates to something very topical, that is to say, the possible—or impossible—articulation between analytic discourse and its outside, which would be political discourse. But it seems that the film remains suspended at that point and can't achieve a resolution of that question.

3 Maurice Blanchot's text 'Détruire' on *Destroy, She Said* appeared in the special issue of *Ça/Cinéma* on Duras published by Éditions Albatros in 1975:

> Where do they come from? Who are they? Certainly beings like ourselves; there are no others in this world. But, in fact, beings already radically destroyed (hence the allusion to Judaism); yet, in such a way that far from leaving unhappy scars, this erosion, this devastation or infinite movement toward death, which lives in them as their only memory of themselves (in one, as the flash of lightning which finally reveals an absence; in another, as a slow, unfinished progression of time; and, in the girl, through her youth, because she is fully destroyed by her absolute relationship to youth), these things liberated them through gentleness, for attention to others, for a non-possessive, unspecified, unlimited love, liberated them for all this and for the singular word that they each carry, having received it from the youngest, the young woman of the night, the one who, alone, can 'say' it with perfect truth: *destroy, she said* (Maurice Blanchot, 'Destroy' in *Marguerite Duras by Marguerite Duras*. San Francisco: City Lights Books, 1987, p. 132).

4 Duras, *Le Camion*, pp. 25 and 74.

5 Reprinted by Gallimard in 2006 as *Le Bureau de poste de la rue Dupin et autres entretiens*.

6 Marguerite Duras, 'Sublime, forcément sublime, Christine V.', *Libération*, 17 July 1985. The body of the child Grégory had been discovered on 16 October 1984.

7 Duras wrote, among other things:

> No man in the world can know what it's like for a woman to be taken by a man she doesn't desire. The woman penetrated without desire is in murder [*dans le meurtre*]. The cadaverous weight of virile *jouissance* above her body has the weight of the murder she doesn't have the strength to deliver back—the weight of madness . . . And that she didn't see the progress of her misfortune is certain; she would have less and less idea where she was going: into a night that would close in on her, the innocent Christine V., who perhaps killed without knowing it, as I write without knowing, her eyes pressed against the windowpane trying to see clearly in the deepening darkness of that October day.

Following the publication of this article, Françoise Sagan, Benoîte Groult, Simone Signoret, Régine Desforges and Angelo Rinaldi were to protest fiercely, while Edmonde Charles-Roux defended her. On 14 November 1986, during an interview with Pierre Bénichou and Hervé Le Masson that appeared in *Le Nouvel Observateur*, she declared: 'I don't give a damn about her crime. The judges don't give a damn about it, I'm sure! At any rate, no one has dared to attack her since my article.' Christine Villemin would refuse to meet Duras and would sue her and the newspaper for defamation, on the grounds that Duras had implied that Villemin was actually a murderer, something she denied. That civil action against *Libération* would fail only in 1994. But the murder charge against Christine Villemin would be dismissed on 3 February 1993 for lack of evidence. In the ensuing years, DNA tests provided no conclusive results, but they resumed again in September 2012 due to the development of new methods of technological investigation. On the very evening that the murder case was dismissed, the France 3 TV channel broadcast on its evening news programme an interview with Duras by Christine Ockrent, recorded a few days before, at a point when dismissal already seemed the virtually certain outcome. Duras persisted with her idea that her analyses in every respect found Christine V. innocent, attributing her murder to her condition as a woman deceived. She also argued that any woman would have found her innocent. But she added that, in order to avoid any misunderstanding and scandal, her article ought to have begun with the precautionary remark, 'If we are in fact talking about a criminal in this case.' She was insisting, then, that her article be read as a mere hypothesis, which retrospectively gave it a quite different meaning. Ockrent asked: 'As you see it, is the affair closed?' She replied: 'This affair is over. I don't know if it is closed. French is a fine language sometimes. It is over.'

8 In 1993 Duras will write a self-defence that employs the same line of argument with regard both to her article and to the affair in general:

> The problem of this crime is a women's problem. The problem of children is a women's problem. The problem of men is a women's problem. Men know nothing about it. So long as men are deluded about the free use of their muscular, material force, deep intelligence will not be a masculine thing. Only women will be aware of men's mistake about themselves. There is something much worse than a slapping for a badly cooked steak, there is daily life.

This text [entitled 'Lettre à Isabelle C.'] was to remain unpublished until it appeared in Laure Adler, *Marguerite Duras* (Paris: Gallimard, 1998), p. 588. [It does not appear to figure in the English translation published in 2000.—Trans.]. Other texts relating to the affair are to be found in the special dossier 'Marguerite Duras, la voix et la passion' [Marguerite Duras, Voice and Passion], edited by Jean-Pierre Martin and published by *Le Monde* in August–October 2012. That dossier also contains the text by Jacques Lacan, an interview with Hélène Cixous and Michel Foucault that had appeared in the *Cahiers Renaud-Barrault* 89 (1975), and contributions from Laure Adler, Jean Vallier, Yann Andréa, Philippe Sollers, Julia Kristeva, Peter Handke, Jeanne Moreau and Didier Eribon.

9 On 17 October 1988, Duras underwent a tracheotomy and remained in hospital for almost a year, after being put into a medically induced coma. Her first detox had taken place in October 1982. It is probably this episode she is alluding to, which was described by Yann Andréa in *M. D.* (Paris: Minuit, 1983).

10 The explosion and fire at the Chernobyl Power Plant in Pripyat, Ukraine, which occurred on 26 April 1986, is generally regarded as one of the worst nuclear disasters in history. [Trans.]

• • • TRAJECTORIES OF WRITING

1 The book by Yann Andréa, whose real surname was Lemée, is, as mentioned above, an account of Duras' treatment for alcoholism.

2 Maurice Blanchot, *The Unavowable Community* (Pierre Joris trans.) (Barrytown: Station Hill Press, 1988), p. 44.

3 Jérôme Lindon was the head of the Éditions de Minuit publishing house from 1948 until his death in 2001 when his daughter Irène succeeded to the post. [Trans.]

4   Jacques Lacan published a homage to this novel in *Cahiers Renaud-Barrault* 52 (December 1965): 7–15. Among other things, he writes:

> Is this not enough to reveal to us what has happened to Lol, and what it says about love; that is, about this image, an image of the self in which the other dresses you and in which you are dressed and which, when you are robbed of it, lets you be just what underneath? What is left to be said about that evening, Lol, in all your passion of nineteen years, so taken with your dress which wore your nakedness, giving it its brilliance?
>
> What you are left with, then, is what they said about you when you were a child, that you were never all there.
>
> But what exactly is this vacuity? It begins to take on a meaning: you were, yes, for one night until dawn, when something in that place gave way, the centre of attention.
>
> What lies concealed in this locution? A centre is not the same on all surfaces. Singular on a flat surface, everywhere on a sphere, on a more complex surface it can produce an odd knot. This last knot is ours.
>
> Because you sense that all this has to do with an envelope having neither an inside nor an outside, and in the seam of its centre every gaze turns back into your own, that these gazes are your own, which your own saturates and which, Lol, you will forever crave from every passerby. Let us follow Lol as she passes from one to the other, seizing from them this talisman which everyone is so eager to cast off: the gaze.

Every gaze will be yours, Lol, as the fascinated Jacques Hold will say to himself, for himself, ready to love 'all of Lol'.

There is in fact a grammar of the subject which has taken note of this stroke of genius. It will return under the pen which pointed it out to me.

You can verify it, this gaze is everywhere in the novel. And the woman of the event is easy to recognize, since Marguerite Duras has depicted her as non-gaze.

I teach that vision splits itself between the image and the gaze, that the first model for the gaze is the stain, from which is derived the radar that the splitting of the eye offers up to the scopic field.

The gaze spreads itself as a stroke on the canvas, making you lower your own gaze before the work of the painter (*Marguerite Duras by Marguerite Duras*, pp. 125–6).

5 *Le ravissement*—this word is enigmatic. Does it have an objective or a subjective dimension—is it a ravishing or a being ravished—as determined by Lol V. Stein?

Ravished. We think of the soul, and of the effect wrought by beauty. But we shall free ourselves, as best we can, from this readily available meaning, by means of a symbol.

A woman who ravishes is also the image imposed on us by this wounded figure, exiled from things, who you dare not touch, but who makes you her prey.

The two movements, however, are knotted together in a cipher that is revealed in a name skilfully crafted in the contour of writing: Lol V. Stein.

Lol V. Stein: paper wings, V, scissors, Stein, stone, in love's guessing game you lose yourself.

One replies: O, open mouth, why do I take three leaps on the water, out of the game of love, where do I plunge?

Such artistry suggests that the ravisher is Marguerite Duras, and we are the ravished. But if, to quicken our steps behind Lol's steps, which resonate through the novel, we were to hear them behind us without having run into anyone, is it then that her creature moves within a space which is doubled; or is it rather that one of us has passed through the other, and which of us, in that case, has let himself be traversed?

Or do we now realize that the cipher is to be calculated in some other way: for to figure it out, one must count *oneself* three (ibid., p. 122).

6   In 1989. She had not yet published *Summer Rain* (1990), *The North China Lover* (1991), *Yann Andréa Steiner* (1992) and *Writing* (1993).

7   On the album *Ha! Ha! Ha!* (1977). The group consisted of John Foxx (vocals), Stevie Shears (guitar), Warren Cann (drums), Chris Cross (bass) and Billy Currie (violin and keyboards).

• • •   TOWARDS A TEXTUAL ANALYSIS

1   *La Princesse de Clèves* was published anonymously in Paris in March 1678. There seems little doubt that its author was Marie-Madeleine Pioche de La Vergne, Comtesse de La Fayette, a member of the minor

French nobility. See Madame de Lafayette, *The Princesse de Clèves* (Terence Cave trans.) (London: Oxford University Press, 2008). Other translations use the English title *The Princess of Cleves* and variant spellings of the author's name. [Trans.]

2   In an interview with Bernard Pivot on the *Apostrophes* programme of 28 September 1984, two months before she was awarded the Prix Goncourt for *The Lover*. She said she was sure she had now achieved this 'flowing writing', having tried for a long time to do so. She defined it as follows: 'an almost absent-minded writing that flows, that's more intent on grasping things than speaking them, you see—I'm talking about the crest of words—that runs along the crest, so as to go quickly, so as not to lose things.'

3   On Duras' death, Jacqueline Risset borrowed this expression for the obituary she published in *L'Unità* in March 1996.

> She has gone to that 'wild land' that writing was for her. Perhaps Marguerite Duras was the one to fulfil, better than the other writers of the twentieth century, Flaubert's desire to 'write a book about nothing', to submit the possibility of the act of writing to the utmost scrutiny, to define what might be called the primary cell, the atom of literature. In her books, fiction comes to life, not as it might seem at first sight through the fullness of the novelistic imaginary, with its rich flourishes, its composite, exotic spaces, but through the thoroughly pared-down, almost totally rarefied basic elements. And each time, it is about the exploration of an unknown space—often love as a site of emptiness and absence.

• • • LITERATURE

1   Marguerite Yourcenar, *With Open Eyes: Conversations with Matthieu Galey* (Arthur Goldhammer trans.) (Boston: Beacon Press, 1984), p. 121.

2   Ibid., p. 195.

3   Nathalie Sarraute, *The Age of Suspicion: Essays on the Novel* (Maria Jolas trans.) (New York: G. Braziller, 1963).

4   Nathalie Sarraute, *Childhood* (Barbara Wright trans.) (New York: G. Braziller, 1985). This was, in reality, Sarraute's first true popular success.

5   Robbe-Grillet was, in fact, in process of writing that volume, *Les Derniers jours de Corinthe* [The Last Days of Corinth], since it would not appear until 1994. The first two volumes, *Le Miroir qui revient* (1985) and *Angélique ou l'Enchantement* (1988), had already appeared, both published by Éditions de Minuit.

6   In a later interview with Irène Frain published in the magazine *Lire* (July–August 2000), Robbe-Grillet was to say: 'At the beginning, she was a funny, warm, lively woman. Towards the end, she became the character swollen with pride that has often been described. Every normal writer has to be convinced he is the greatest. Marguerite Duras was no exception to that rule, but she was simply unable to imagine that other writers than her were too ...'

7   Philippe Sollers was to publish an article in *Le Nouvel Observateur* of 3–9 February 1994 entitled 'Duras médium'. This was reprinted in Sollers, *Éloge de l'infini* (Paris: Gallimard, 2001) and in the special dossier of *Le Monde* entitled *Marguerite Duras, la voix et la passion* [Marguerite Duras, Voice and Passion], p. 85. He wrote:

> Duras' books are incantations, litanies, gnomic utterances, divine afflatus. And afterwards, on the stage, who is

spellbinding whom? Television? Marguerite Duras? Where
is the truth? Where is the power?'

Some years later, he will grant a fascinating, very frank interview to
Jean-François Kervéan on the antipathy that had developed between
Duras and himself in *L'Événement du jeudi* of 2 September 1998 on the
occasion of Laure Adler's biography of Duras being published. Among
other things, Sollers says:

> The Duras problem interests me because she is the charac-
> ter emblematic of a France I don't recognize myself in . . .
> With her we are, at the beginning, in the first great French
> problem which is that of colonialism—in this case in
> Indochina. And we have a Marguerite Duras who, under the
> name Donnadieu, presents herself as the champion of
> French colonialism. Her book at the time is explicit on this
> . . . She's an able writer, with considerable powers of reve-
> lation in the sense in which a medium makes 'revelations'.
> Her literature is more of the order of a soothsayer's utter-
> ances than a conscious exercise of language. There's a force
> in her, from which she derives her hypnotic hold which,
> when transferred to the screen in *India Song* or *Hiroshima
> mon amour*, reaches such a degree of ridicule and pathos
> that a mere child could jump up and point out that the
> emperor has no clothes. I'd suggest a relationship here
> between a hieratic style of behaviour and a way of hypno-
> tizing oneself and a whole country that's quite something
> . . . What I hear in Duras is something powerful, very insis-
> tent, authoritarian and instrumentalized, but something
> which, to my ear at least, sounds bogus . . . I've always
> wondered where this sense of the bogus comes from.

Let's go on . . . Then she got into what shocked me most, which I shall call pseudo-Judaism. I'm very sorry that I hear it this way, but in her proclaimed philosemitism, you can detect an over-commitment which, in my view, is due to an intense sense of guilt on her part for not having recognized the scale of the Holocaust. That guilt induces a self-terrorization that consists in trying to play the Jew in the Jews' stead. That was how it was with Duras . . . In the 1970s we used to see each other. *Tel Quel* was near the rue Saint-Benoît and we'd go for a coffee at the Pré-aux-Clercs. She was quite positive towards me. That was the period of feminism too . . . She was relatively nice. She must already have been drinking a lot, but no matter. Then came the explosion, with the publication of [Sollers's novel] *Women*. The book made a big impact. That was the point when she was about to hit the headlines, a year later, with *The Lover*. Mitterand came to power and she became the Sybil of the Elysée Palace, its prophetess . . . She embarked on her extraordinary ministry, in which she pronounced on Africa, the French provinces, the sex organ of the recumbent statue of Victor Noir in the Père Lachaise cemetery . . . This is the time of the Duras–Mitterand conversations in *L'Autre Journal*. She congratulates Mitterand on having built the submarine *Richelieu*, to which he politely points out that it's an aircraft carrier. But no matter, these were the days of the soar-away Duras act . . . In an interview she did with Pierre Bergé for *Globe*, I was portrayed as the monk on the 'Chaussée aux moines' cheese label—tonsured, risible, vile with women, a talentless novelist, etc. From that point on, her attacks became systematic. After *Women*, she saw

me as a blight on the landscape and hence to be destroyed
. . . There's a coldness and hardness in her, personally, I
find her sham transcendence forced. I think it's sad that
someone who describes herself as a specialist in love should
ask herself the question Laure Adler reports: 'Why am I so
nasty?' . . . I find her books powerful and hypnotic. But I
think they will age badly. Her films are already nowhere
to be seen. The books will meet the same fate some day or
other. It's a literature that, with all its repetition, seems
artificial and bloated. I always sensed a will to dominate in
her, even on the telephone. I don't like that. I can't imagine
Kafka was like that.

8 Colette Fellous organized a meeting between Jean-Luc Godard and
Duras on 2 December 1987. That one-hour conversation was filmed
by Jean-Daniel Verhaeghe and broadcast as part of the *Océaniques*
programme on FR3 on 28 December 1987. They talked about *Emily
L.* and Godard's film *Soigne ta droite*. Part of the conversation was
published in *Le Magazine littéraire* of June 1990.

9 Duras also bore a grudge against Sartre because, as she relates in
an interview with Edda Melon that was published as a preface to the
Italian translation of *L'Amante anglaise*, he had criticized 'Madame
Dodin' which she had sent him for publication in *Les Temps modernes*.

Sartre called me in to tell me the subject was interesting,
that it was a good story, but I didn't know how to write. And
he added, 'It's not me saying that, but a woman, a woman
I trust implicitly.' It was, of course, Simone de Beauvoir.
And to think that she was such a lousy writer, without the
slightest grace, writing things in which everything is
stated, is already present in the words on the page.

But *Les Temps modernes* did actually publish Duras' short story in May 1952. And it appeared two years later in *Des journées entières dans les arbres*, published by Gallimard.

10 The publisher of the three aforementioned writers. He would, in fact, also be Duras' Italian publisher.

11 Elsa Morante's novel appeared in Italy in 1974, but only in 1977 in France. Morante died on 25 November 1985. [It was published in English translation as *History* in 1977. —Trans.]

• • • A GALLERY OF CHARACTERS

1 Yourcenar, *With Open Eyes*, p. 48. In her text, Yourcenar speaks of Hadrian and Zeno, the central protagonist of *The Abyss*. Later, arguing along the same lines, she will say of her own father, Michel, as depicted in *How Many Years: A Memoir*:

> I am not Michel any more than I am Zeno or Hadrian. I tried to recreate him—as any novelist would—out of my own substance, but that substance is undifferentiated. One nourishes one's created characters with one's own substance: it's rather like the process of gestation. To give the character life, or to give him back life, it is, of course, necessary to fortify him by contributing something of one's own humanity, but it doesn't follow from that that the character is I, the writer, or that I am the character. The two entities remain distinct (ibid., p. 176).

2 Male characters from *The Vice Consul*, *The Sea Wall*, *The Ravishing of Lol V. Stein*, *Moderato Cantabile* and the cycle *L'Amour*, *La Femme du Gange* and *India Song*, respectively.

1   On 29 May 1985, a few minutes before the beginning of the European Cup final between Juventus of Turin and Liverpool, a wall on the terraces and metal fencing collapsed under pressure from Scottish hooligans attacking the Italian supporters, resulting in thirty-nine dead and six hundred injured. Duras wasn't the only one in front of her television. The whole of Europe watched this barbarism live. [It isn't clear why the Heysel disaster is ascribed by the French translator to *Scottish* hooligans, nor indeed why he fails to mention that the Belgian courts attributed blame for this event in a more complex way. —Trans.]

2   Nine years later, on 4 March 1996, the footballer confided to the journalist Patrick Leroux, also in *Libération*:

> That interview felt completely unreal, or rather surreal, insofar as I didn't know who Marguerite Duras was, I wasn't aware of her intellectual reputation. No, I wasn't overawed since I'd no idea of the importance of this person in a literary world I knew nothing or virtually nothing about. On the other hand, I was very interested to meet her, since I've always loved getting to meet people from outside the football world. She fitted the bill, because I'm sure she'd never been to a football match. What I remember of the interview is her approach to me as a player. She kept talking about angelism, she'd even invented a word, *angélhomme* [angelman], to describe footballers. She saw me as a blue angel ... It was funny, it was new, and it was a completely different way of seeing sport. She talked to me a lot about atmosphere, about the relations between man and ball and about my family. Her questions were often affecting. When I played in Italy, a number of writers had written long articles on me, but they were all intellectuals who were interested

in football. I was never questioned before by someone who knew so little about the game.

3 'Duras-Platini, le stade de l'ange'. This was a meeting organized by the journalist Jean-Pierre Delacroix to coincide with the publication of Michel Platini's book *Ma vie comme un match* (in collaboration with Patrick Mahé. Paris: Laffont, 1987). It was filmed as a two-part televised interview, 'Qu'est-ce que c'est que ce jeu-là. Démoniaque et divin' (14 December) and 'Le Stade de l'ange' (15 December), the two parts being broadcast as part of the programme *Des idées et des hommes*. Among other things, Duras said:

> My job in the world is to look at it. The football pitch is a place where the other is the equal of yourself. On an equal footing . . . The football pitch, that place where the players play, to which they are confined, is a theatre the spectators watch, a place of confrontation and hence a place that's already political. As soon as you have something at stake, even something like a banal victory, then defeat is also at stake, which is already less banal—and its justification through the use of insult: you're no longer playing for the sake of playing, you're playing against an enemy. And all's fair in trying to do them down and give grounds for their defeat. No one escapes this abomination. Of course, there's no translation into politics of what happens in a stadium. But already there's a reflection, a racism—any words are OK. But you've never rejected anyone, I'm sure of that.

This interview was adapted for the theatre by Guy Naigeon in October 2012 at the Nouveau Théâtre du 8ème in Lyon.

4 Co-directed with Paul Seban. Her first film in the strict sense was *Détruire dit-elle* in 1969.

5 Duras, 'Notes on India Song' in *Marguerite Duras by Marguerite Duras*, p. 8 (translation modified).

6 In reality fifteen, if we count the film that was co-directed, the medium-length films and the companion film to *India Song* that is *Son nom de Venise dans Calcutta désert*, which has the same soundtrack but different visuals. To these should be added four shorts. We may, of course, regard *The Long Absence* and *Hiroshima mon amour* as films by Marguerite Duras, since they very much bear her stamp. Her last film, inspired by her text *Ah! Ernesto*, is *The Children* (1985). Most of her films have also been published in written form either before or after the film was made. Several have appeared as small volumes. Duras' stories and novels number somewhere around twenty.

7 Robert Musil, *The Man Without Qualities* (Sophie Wilkins and Burton Pike trans) (London: Picador, 1995), p. 709.

8 Around 200,000 euros in today's money.

9 To Michelle Porte, in *Les Lieux de Marguerite Duras*, p. 94, Duras said:

> But the films that I do make are made in the same place as my books, *the place of passion; it's where one is deaf and blind.* At least I try to be there as much as possible. Whereas the films of the Saturday cinema, as I call it, the cinema of the consumer society, which are meant to please, to amuse, are *made in the place of the spectator,* following precise formulae certain to appeal to him, to keep him there the length of the show. But this cinema, once it is ended, leaves nothing, nothing after it. It is erased the moment it's through. While mine, *it seems to me, begins the next day, like something read* ('The Places of Marguerite Duras', Edith Cohen trans., *Enclitic* 7[2] [Fall 1983]: 60).

10 None of Duras' films has been as successful as her books. Her son Jean Mascolo bought up the rights to the eleven full-length films for the Éditions Benoît Jacob which he founded in 1998, in order to make available his mother's forgotten (literary and cinematographic) works or those which had become hard to find. Gérard Depardieu bought the footage of *Le Camion*.

11 In *Le Monde* of 27 November 1981, Duras published a warning—or, rather, an instruction—to the public, aimed at those who might not be prepared to tolerate the half hour of absolute darkness the film contained. It recommended that those viewers 'completely avoided seeing *L'Homme atlantique* and, in fact, gave it a very wide berth'. As for the 'others', they 'should see it without fail and not miss it for anything'.

12 This radical, and in fact caricatural, position probably doesn't reflect the relationship between the two artists, who have many things in common, as is often highlighted in academic studies. The ignorance of Pasolini which Duras professes here was probably not always so clear-cut. It seems unthinkable that she didn't see *The Hawks and the Sparrows* [*Uccellacci e uccellini*], which ties in with her obsessions about the Communist Party, or *Medea*, which was so close to her conception of passion and, most importantly, had Maria Callas in it whom she venerated—not to mention such films as *Pigsty*, *The Earth as Seen from the Moon* [*La Terra vista dalla Luna*] or *Teorema*, which have an aesthetic form and use symbolism in a way that could not but be of direct interest to her. We can only deplore that she did not read Pasolini's *The Scent of India* and his political poems from the 1960s and 70s, which coincide with her concerns at that time. Similarly, her peremptory condemnation of Ingmar Bergman below may also seem aberrant. Or Duras' injunction against the use of speech in the cinema, which is more than somewhat paradoxical coming from her.

13 'L'homme tremblant. Conversation entre Marguerite Duras et Elia Kazan', *Cahiers du Cinéma* 318 (December 1980). Reprinted in *Les Yeux verts* (Paris: Cahiers du cinéma, 1987), p. 193.

14 Among other things, she told him:

> I am like you. I was born in the colonies. The place of my birth was demolished. And, if you like, that's always with me—the fact of not living where you were born... You had two strokes of luck. Poverty and the distance from the place where you lived afterwards. I view that as two strokes of luck. You were able to go back to Turkey. For me, there was the war, I was married, I had a child, I've never been able to go back to my native country and I never will. I'm completely separated from my childhood (ibid.).

15 *Les Cahiers du cinéma* 312–13 (June 1980, special issue edited by Serge Daney). Translated by Carol Barko as *Green Eyes* (New York: Columbia University Press, 1990).

16 In 1987. It was reprinted in 2006.

17 The *Cahiers du Cinéma* organized a round-table discussion on the film, in which Godard actually said 'Let's begin by saying that it's great literature' (without mentioning Duras) and, in reality, concentrated mainly on Resnais's cinematographic work:

> There's one things that troubles me a bit in *Hiroshima*, which also troubled me in *Night and Fog* and it's that there's a certain readiness to show horrific scenes, since we're quickly beyond aesthetics here. I mean that, whether they're filmed well or badly—that doesn't much matter—such scenes make a dreadful impression on the viewer. Whether a film about concentration camps or torture bears the name of Couzinet or Visconti, I find personally that it

makes very little difference. Before *Brink of Life*, there was a documentary produced by UNESCO which showed in a montage with a musical accompaniment, all the people who were suffering on the earth—the disabled, the blind, the infirm, the hungry, the old, the young, etc.—the title escapes me. It must have been called *Man* or something of that kind. Well, the film was vile. No comparison with *Night and Fog*, but all the same it was a film that was disturbing to people, just as recently the *Nuremberg Trials* were. The trouble then, in showing scenes of horror, is that you're automatically outstripped by your intentions, and people are shocked by these images in more or less the same way as they are by pornographic images. Ultimately, what shocks me in Hiroshima is that the images of the couple making love in the early shots frighten me the same way as the images of the wounds—also in close-up—caused by the atomic bomb. There's something not immoral, but amoral in showing love or horror with the same close-ups like that. That's perhaps where Resnais is truly modern as opposed to someone like Rossellini. But I also find that it's a regression, since in *Journey to Italy*, when George Sanders and Ingrid Bergman are looking at the charred bodies of the couple in Pompeii, you had the same sense of anguish and beauty, but with something extra (Jean Domarchi, Jacques Doniol-Valcroze, Jean-Luc Godard, Pierre Kast, Jacques Rivette and Éric Rohmer, 'Table ronde sur *Hiroshima mon amour* d'Alain Resnais', *Cahiers du cinema* 97 [July 1959]. Reprinted in Luc Lagier, *Hiroshima mon amour: Duras écrit et Resnais filme*. Paris: Cahiers du Cinéma/SCÉRÉN-CNDP, 2007).

18 In fact, Resnais went to Japan merely to make the film once the screenplay had been written. It was during the making of the film that he requested one-off changes from Duras, but he sometimes had to make changes without waiting for her agreement. In Luc Lagier's book (see note 17 above), the article Duras published in *France-Observateur* is cited ('Travailler pour le cinéma', August 1958):

> I didn't have the time in nine weeks to produce literature, as Resnais very well knew. Just as he knew I hadn't the time to produce a screenplay, that I didn't know how. Yet he continued to advise me to be literary. Up to the last day that was his advice. If we had to save the face of something during this period, Resnais had chosen to save the literary face of the enterprise.

In an interview published in *Le Monde* on 9 November 1972, Duras is more precise. She wrote a synopsis in a fortnight. Resnais approved it and in the seven weeks preceding his leaving for Japan they worked together: 'Each day I developed the synopsis. Resnais came every day or every other day to read what I'd written. Either he "could see" it or he couldn't and when he couldn't I started again until he could. Then he asked me to describe the film to him as though it were done.'

19 The equivalent of 30,000 euros at today's rates.

20 This is the nickname Duras gave to her son Jean.

21 Respectively in *Nathalie Granger* (Jeanne Moreau and Lucia Bosè), *India Song* (Delphine Syrig), *Whole Days in the Trees* (Bulle Ogier and Madeleine Renaud), *Agatha and the Limitless Readings* (Bulle Ogier), *Le Navire Night* (Dominique Sanda), *Jaune le soleil* and *Woman of the Ganges* (Catherine Sellers). Isabelle Adjani, the partner of Bruno Nuytten, who was Duras' cinematographer, was simply a close friend and never worked with her.

22 The play was premiered at the Odéon on 1 December 1965 in a production by Jean-Louis Barrault and had a second run ten years later, beginning on 14 October 1975, at the Théâtre d'Orsay.

23 In 1969 Duras published a portrait entitled 'Delphine Seyrig, a Celebrated Unknown', which was republished in *Outside: Selected Writings* (Arthur Goldhammer trans.) (London: Fontana, 1987), pp. 159–63.

24 Duras also devoted an article/interview to Jeanne Moreau in *Vogue* in 1965, which is reprinted in *Outside* (pp. 164–72). Let us remind the reader that Moreau also starred in *The Sailor from Gibraltar* (1967), that she made a record inspired by *India Song* and that she played Marguerite Duras in the film that was made by Josée Dayan in 2001 from Yann Andréa's book *Cet amour-là*.

● ● ● THEATRE

1 The supplement to the weekly magazine *L'Illustration*, which contained a stage play.

2 Dionys Mascolo (1916–97) was married to Marguerite Duras from 1947 to 1956 and is the father of her son. He worked as a publisher with Gallimard. After a brief period in the French Communist Party, he was an anti-colonial activist. He is the author of several works of non-fiction, including *Le Communisme* (Paris: Gallimard, 1953) and *Autour d'un effet de mémoire* (Paris: Nadeau, 1998).

● ● ● PASSION

1 In *With Open Eyes*, Yourcenar deplores, above all, that the European novel ignores the sacred dimension of love, which is almost always presented as 'love born of vanity' (p. 54).

2 Marguerite Duras, *Hiroshima mon amour and Une Aussi Longue Absence* (London: Calder & Boyars, 1966), p. 25.

3 In *Hiroshima mon amour*, 'she' says on the same page: 'Devour me. Deform me to the point of ugliness'.

4 Marguerite Duras, *A Duras Trilogy* (London: John Calder, 1977), p. 91.

5 Marguerite Duras, *The Little Horses of Tarquinia* (Peter DuBerg trans.) (London: John Calder, 1960), p. 161. In the same novel, Sara also says: 'If you only like to make love with one man, you don't like to make love at all' (p. 34). Diana says: 'Any love experienced is a diminution of love' (p. 84).

6 Marguerite Duras, *Moderato Cantabile* in *Four Novels: The Square, Moderato Cantabile, 10:30 on a Summer Night, The Afternoon of Mr. Andesmas* (Richard Seaver trans.) (New York: Grove Press, 1982), p. 118. It is Chauvin's last line of dialogue in the novel.

7 In her interview with Pierre Bénichou and Hervé Le Masson cited above (*Le Nouvel Observateur*, 14 November 1986), Duras declared: 'It isn't fucking that counts, it's having desire. The number of people who fuck without desire, that's already enough as it is. All these women writers talk about it so badly, whereas it's a whole world suddenly before you! I've known since childhood that the world of sexuality was fabulous, tremendous. The rest of my life has only confirmed that.'

8 I acquired that drinker's face before I drank. Drink only confirmed it. The space for it existed in me. I knew it the same as other people, but, strangely, in advance. Just as the space existed in me for desire. At the age of fifteen I had the face of pleasure, and yet I had no knowledge of pleasure. There was no mistaking that face. Even my mother must have seen it. My brothers did. That was how everything started for me—with that flagrant, exhausted face, those rings round the eyes, in advance of time and experience' (Marguerite Duras, *The Lover*. London: Harper Perennial, 2006, p. 12).

9   We find allusions to these experiences in *Blue Eyes, Black Hair*, pp. 77–8.

10 Among other places, in her interview with Jérôme Beaujour: 'The men are homosexuals. All men are potentially homosexuals—all that's missing is awareness of the fact, an incident or revelation that will bring it home to them. Homosexuals themselves know this and say so. And women who've known homosexuals and really loved them know it and say so too' (Marguerite Duras and and Jérôme Beaujour, *Practicalities: Marguerite Duras Speaks to Jérôme Beaujour*. New York: Grove Weidenfeld, 1990, p. 33). This takes up again what the man tells the woman in *Blue Eyes, Black Hair*: 'He prophesies: Sooner or later he would have come to us, they all come, all one has to do is wait' (p. 69).

11 In Duras and Beaujour, *Practicalities*: 'But in homosexual love the passion is homosexuality itself. What a homosexual loves, as if it were his lover, his country, his art, his land, is homosexuality' (p. 35).

12 Duras has made some very contradictory declarations on this question, which was a very personal concern for her, given her relations with Yann Andréa. Without going back over *The Malady of Death* and *Blue Eyes, Black Hair*, at the centre of which is precisely her passion for a homosexual who has come into her life and the way she turns a sense of deep humiliation into excessive pride, we may recall the text in *Green Eyes* in which she compares feminists and gay activists:

> I see a relation between homosexuality and women's movements. They are, similarly, first and foremost preoccupied with themselves. Even pointless remarks made against homosexuality have the effect of strengthening their position in this minority separatism, paradoxically painful and desired. Today, one could say that women are intent upon still keeping intact and whole their difference with men. In the same way that homosexuals want to stick to the old

tyranny, to keep the whole distance between them and society. To dare to suggest that things are improving for them is to offend them greatly. Like women, homosexuals want to keep open the legal actions brought against man, against society. They institute these actions, they make them the context for belonging, the chosen context of their martyrdom' (*Green Eyes*. Carol Barko trans., New York: Columbia University Press, 1990, pp. 140–1).

13 In 1989 only this book had appeared. After Duras' death, Yann Andréa published *Cet amour-là* (Paris: Pauvert, 1999); *Ainsi* (Paris: Pauvert, 2000) ; and *Dieu commence chaque matin* (Paris: Bayard, 2001).

• • • A WOMAN

1 Duras and Beaujour, *Practicalities*, p. 125.

2 'It seems she said, "My head's full of dizziness and shouting. Full of wind. So, sometimes, for example, I write. Pages, you see." ' (Duras, *Le Camion*, p. 35.)

3 Mitterand held this ministerial post from 21 October 1947 to 19 July 1948 in the government of Paul Ramadier and the first Robert Schuman government, both under the presidency of Vincent Auriol.

4   It is natural for the sexes to co-operate. One has a profound, if irrational, instinct in favour of the theory that the union of man and woman makes for the greatest satisfaction, the most complete happiness. But the sight of the two people getting into the taxi and the satisfaction it gave me made me also ask whether there are two sexes in the mind corresponding to the two sexes in the body, and whether they also require to be united in order to get complete satisfaction and happiness? And I went on amateurishly to sketch

a plan of the soul so that in each of us two powers preside, one male, one female; and in the man's brain the man pre-dominates over the woman, and in the woman's brain the woman predominates over the man. The normal and com-fortable state of being is that when the two live in harmony together, spiritually co-operating (Virginia Woolf, *A Room of One's Own*. London: Vintage Books, 2001, p. 84.)

5 Duras is borrowing words from Samuel Taylor Coleridge which follow the preceding quotation in Woolf's text.

If one is a man, still the woman part of his brain must have effect; and a woman also must have intercourse with the man in her. Coleridge perhaps meant this when he said that a great mind is androgynous. It is when this fusion takes place that the mind is fully fertilized and uses all its faculties.

Woolf herself develops a long analysis of the androgyny of every cre-ative mind. The exact quotation from Coleridge, which dates from 1 September 1832 in his posthumously published *Table Talk*, is as follows:

I have known strong minds with imposing, undoubting, Cobbett-like manners, but I have never met a great mind of this sort. And of the former, they are at least as often wrong as right. The truth is, a great mind must be andro-gynous. Great minds—Swedenborg's for instance—are never wrong but in consequence of being in the right, but imperfectly.

6 While the man is hunting and fighting, the woman works with her wits, with her imagination: she brings forth dreams and gods. On certain days she becomes a seeress, borne on boundless wings of reverie and desire. The better

to reckon up the seasons, she watches the sky; but her heart belongs to earth none the less. Young and flower-like herself, she looks down toward the enamoured flowers, and forms with them a personal acquaintance. As a woman, she beseeches them to heal the objects of her love (Michelet, 'Introduction' in *La Sorcière: The Witch of the Middle Ages.* Lionel J. Trotter trans., London: Simpkin, Marshall and Co., 1883).

7 Dionys Mascolo, 'Birth of Tragedy' in *Marguerite Duras by Marguerite Duras*, p. 140.

8 In an interview with Mathilde de la Bardonnie published in *Libération* on 18 August 1998, two years after his mother's death and a year after the death of his father, Jean Mascolo was to say: 'I adored my mother and she adored me for forty-nine years. Even if we were often a pair of terrors. My father was my best friend. She taught me freedom, how to preserve a wildness and, most importantly, how to cook.'

• • • PLACES

1 This began life as a film (of 1976) directed by Michelle Porte. It was transcribed and published as a book by Éditions de Minuit in 1978.

2 Marie Donnadieu, née Legrand, died on 23 August 1956 after the publication of *The Sea Wall* and *Whole Days in the Trees*, but long before Duras had written of the Chinese lover. In a 1988 text published in the collective volume edited by Marcel Bisiaux and Catherine Jajolet, *A ma mère. 60 écrivains parlent de leur mère* (Paris: Éditions Pierre Horay, 1988) and reprinted in *Le Monde extérieur* (Paris: POL, 1993), she writes:

I believe I loved my mother more than anything, and that ended all of a sudden. I think it was when I had my child. Or, also, when the film made from *The Sea Wall* [René

Clément's 1958 film, *This Angry Age*] came out. After that
she didn't want to see me. In the end, she let me visit her,
though she said 'You should have waited till I died.' I didn't
understand, thinking she was just being awkward, but that
wasn't it at all. What we believed to be entirely praiseworthy
in her, she saw only as her failure. It was a complete break
and I gave up trying to make it up with her because I
couldn't see any possible grounds for an understanding.
Other instances of discord followed.

After the publication of *Whole Days in the Trees*, Duras never saw her
mother again until she died.

3   Published in serial form in *Libération* every Wednesday over two
months from 16 July to 17 September 1980. It was collected into a single
volume by Éditions de Minuit in 1982.

4   In the album *La Mer écrite* (Paris: Marval, 1996), published in the month
following her death, Duras provides a commentary to photographs by
Hélène Bamberger. These are texts from the summer of 1994, edited
by Yann Andréa.

5   The film *Nathalie Granger* was shot at the house in Neauphle.

'*Le Square*: un roman de Marguerite Duras était conçu comme une pièce', interview by Henri Marc, *Franc-Tireur* (14 September 1956).

'Rendez-vous dans un Square avec Marguerite Duras', interview by Claude Sarraute, *Le Monde* (18 September 1956).

'Non, je ne suis pas la femme d'Hiroshima', interview by André Bourin, *Les Nouvelles littéraires* (18 June 1959).

Interview by Marcel Frère, *Cinéma 60* (February 1960).

'C'est la Seine-et-Oise qui est coupable . . .', interview by Nicole Zand, *Le Monde* (22 February 1963).

Interview by Madeleine Chapsal, *L'Express*. Reprinted in Madeleine Chapsal, *Quinze écrivains* (Paris: Julliard, 1963) and in *Ces voix que j'entends encore* (Paris: Fayard, 2011).

'Les hommes d'aujourd'hui ne sont pas assez féminins', interview by Pierre Hahn, *Lettres et Médecins* (March 1964).

'Une journée étouffante', interview by C. M., *La Gazette de Lausanne* (19–20 September 1964).

'Une interview de Marguerite Duras', by Jacques Vivien, *Paris-Normandie* (2 April 1965).

'L'Amour est un devenir constant comme la révolution', interview by Yvonne Baby, *Le Monde* (7 March 1967).

'*L'Amante anglaise* ou la chimie de la folie', interview by Claude Sarraute, Le *Monde* (20 December 1968).

'*Détruire, dit-elle*, lu par Pierre Dumayet, commenté par Marguerite Duras', *Le Monde* (5 April 1969).

'La folie me donne de l'espoir', interview by Yvonne Baby, *Le Monde* (17 December 1969).

'Marguerite Duras tourne *India Song*: texte, théâtre, film', interview by Colette Godard, *Le Monde* (28 July 1974).

'Parce que le silence est féminin', interview by Pierre Bregstein, *Cinématographe* 13 (May–June 1975).

'*Son nom de Venise dans Calcutta désert*', interview by Claire Clouzot, *Écran* 49 (July–August 1976).

'Je ne me laisserai pas récupérer', interview by Anne de Gasperi, *Les Nouvelles littéraires* (25 November 1976).

Interview by Anne de Gasperi, *Le Quotidien de Paris* (8 January 1977).

'Le feu d'artifice de Marguerite Duras', interview by Jack Gousseland, *Le Point* (14 February 1977).

'Le désir est bradé, saccagé', interview by Michèle Manceaux, *Marie-Claire* 297 (May 1977).

'Le Noir atlantique', *Des Femmes en mouvement* 57 (11 September 1981).

'Le décor de *Savannah Bay*', interview by Roberto Plate, *Cahiers Renaud-Barrault* 106 (September 1983).

'L'Attente du père', interview by François Peraldi, *Études freudiennes* 23 (1984).

'C'est fou c'que j'peux t'aimer: entretien de Marguerite Duras avec Yann Andréa', interview by Didier Eribon, *Libération* (4 January 1984).

'Ils n'ont pas trouvé de raisons de me le refuser', interview by Marianne Alphant, *Libération* (13 November 1984).

'Duras-Zouc, entretien avec Zouc', *Le Monde* (13 December 1984; in this case, Duras is the interviewer).

'Comment ne pas être effrayée par cette masse fabuleuse de lecteurs?', interview by Pierre Assouline, *Lire* 112 (January 1985). Reprinted in Pierre Assouline, *Écrire, Lire et en parler* (Paris: Laffont, 1985).

'Duras tout entière . . . Un entretien avec un écrivain au-dessus de tout Goncourt', interview by Pierre Bénichou and Hervé Le Masson, *Le Nouvel Observateur* (14–20 November 1986).

'Marguerite Duras: "La littérature est illégale ou elle n'est pas"', interview by Gilles Costaz, *Le Matin* (14 November 1986).

'Marguerite Duras par Anne Sinclair', interview by Anne Sinclair, *Elle* 8 (December 1986).

'Au peigne fin', interview by André Rollin, *Lire* 136 (January 1987).

'L'exacte exactitude de Denis Belloc', *Libération* (19–20 September 1987; Duras is the interviewer).

Interviews with Michel Platini, *Libération* (14 and 15 December 1987; Duras is the interviewer).

'Duras dans les régions claires de l'écriture', interview by Colette Fellous, *Le Journal littéraire* (December 1987).

'L'ultima immagine del mondo', interview by Edda Melon, 18 February 1988. Published in Italian in the new edition of the translation of *L'Amante anglaise* (Feltrinelli, 1988).

'La vie Duras', interview by Marianne Alphant, *Libération* (11 January 1990).

'Duras parle du nouveau Duras' (on *La Pluie d'été*), interview by Pierrette Rosset, *Elle* 2297 (5 January 1990).

'J'ai vécu le réel comme un mythe', interview by Aliette Armel, *Le Magazine littéraire* (June 1990).

'Duras dans le parc à amants', interview by Marianne Alphant, *Libération* (13 June 1991).

'Vous faites une différence entre mes livres et mes films?', interview by Jean-Michel Frodon and Danièle Heymann, *Le Monde* (13 June 1991).

'Les nostalgies de l'amante Duras' (on *Yann Andréa Steiner*), interview by Jean-Louis Ezine, *Le Nouvel Observateur* (24 June–1 July 1992).